History for NI Key Stage

Ireland

1169–1500

● Sheelagh Dean ● Cheryl Stafford ● Catherine Thompson

Hodder Murray

A MEMBER OF THE HODDER HEADLINE GROUP

The Publishers would like to acknowledge the use of the following textual extracts:

Acknowledgements

p.12 Extract from 'Bloody lesson that was well learned', *The Times*, 1 July 2006; **p.27** (Source 4) Extract from *Ireland and the Normans: Progress or Decline?*, Dr. Brendan Smith, Longman, 1993; **p.63** (Source 3) Extract from *Ireland in the Middle Ages*, Sean Duffy, Palgrace Macmillan, 1997; **p.70** (Source 7) Extract from *Medieval Realms*, John Aylett, Hodder & Stoughton, 1991.

Every effort has been made to trace all copyright holders, but if any have been inadvertently overlooked the Publishers will be pleased to make the necessary arrangements at the first opportunity.

The Publishers would like to thank the following for permission to reproduce copyright material:

Photo credits

p.6 *t* © Crawford Municipal Art Gallery, Cork, Ireland/The Bridgeman Art Library, *bl* courtesy Portadown District L.O.L. No. 1, *br* AP/Empics; **p.7** *t* Popperfoto.com, *bl* Philip Wolmuth/Alamy, *br* By permission of the British Library (MS Royal 13 B. VIII, f.22); **p.13** © Stephane Reix/For Picture/Corbis; **p.16** Joe Tree/Alamy; **p.17** Peter Dazeley/Alamy; **p.18** *t* © Sean Adair/Reuters/Corbis, *b* Courtesy NIAS (photo by John McPoland); **p.19** *t* Reuters/Str Old, *c* Getty Images, *b* Rex Features; **p.21** *tr* Reproduced courtesy of Hastings Direct; **p.26** Michael Jenner/Alamy; **p.38** Icon of St Laurence O'Toole by Sr. Aloysius McVeigh R.S.M., reproduced courtesy of Parish of St Kevin's, Glendalough, Co. Wicklow; **p.57** argus/Still Pictures; **p.62** © Geray Sweeney/Corbis; **p.69** TopFoto/The British Library/HIP; **p.70** © Ecole nationale supérieure des beaux-arts Paris/Giraudon/Bridgeman Art Library; **p.78** TopFoto/HIP; **p.79** TopFoto/The British Library/HIP; **p.82** Culliganphoto/Alamy; **p.83** *t* David Lyons/Alamy, *b* © Alain Le Garsmeur/Collections; **p.84** David Lyons/Alamy; **p.89** David Lyons/Alamy.

Orders: please contact Bookpoint Ltd, 130 Milton Park, Abingdon, Oxon OX14 4SB. Telephone: (44) 01235 827720. Fax: (44) 01235 400454. Lines are open 9.00 – 5.00, Monday to Saturday, with a 24-hour message answering service. Visit our website at www.hoddereducation.co.uk

© Dean, Stafford and Thompson 2007
First published in 2007 by
Hodder Murray, an imprint of Hodder Education,
a member of the Hodder Headline Group
an Hachette Livre UK company,
338 Euston Road
London NW1 3BH

Impression number	5	4	3	2	
Year	2011	2010	2009	2008	2007

Cover photo: The Norman castle at Carrickfergus, Co. Antrim, Ireland.
© Christopher Hill/Irish Image Collection
Illustrations by Richard Duszczak and Oxford Designers and Illustrators
Typeset in Imperial. Layouts by Fiona Webb
Printed in Italy

A catalogue record for this title is available from the British Library

ISBN-13: 978 0340 814 833

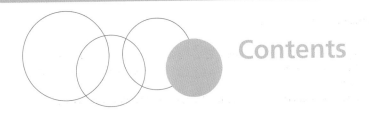

Contents

Introduction – what this book is about

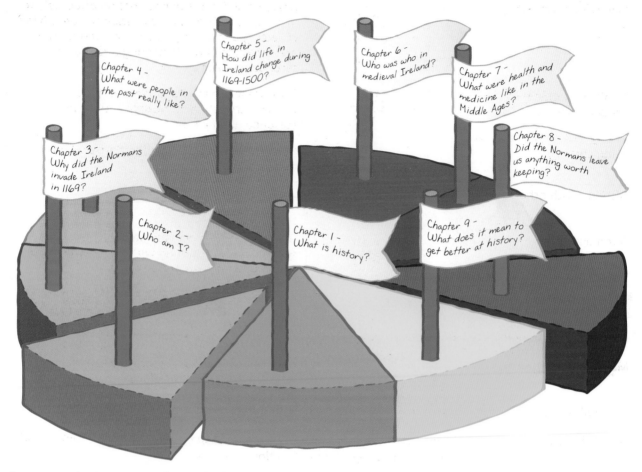

As you make your way through this book, you will start to develop the skills you need to be good at and enjoy history. The nine flags above show the chapter titles in the book, each of which asks a big question.

FEATURES OF THE BOOK

In Chapters 1–8 you will find:

- **Learning intentions.** These tell you the skills and knowledge you will be learning in the chapter.

- **Thinking skills and personal capabilities icons.** These show you at a glance where you have the opportunity to develop some cross-curricular skills. These icons are explained in the table opposite.

- **Get Active.** These are tasks which help you improve your thinking and practise your skills in history.

- **Plan, Do, Review.** This helps you pull together all your work at the end of the chapter and gives you the opportunity to reflect on your own performance.

- **Key words.** These are highlighted in small capitals and are defined in a glossary at the back of the book (see page 95).

The last chapter in the book, Chapter 9, asks you to reflect on all the skills you have developed throughout Year 8 and to construct your own skills ladder, which you can return to in Year 9.

KEY ELEMENTS

Throughout your Key Stage 3 History course, you will also study aspects of the past which help develop your understanding of the key elements of the curriculum, as shown in the table opposite.

Skill/Capability	Icon	Description
Managing information		Research and manage information effectively to investigate historical issues, including identifying, collecting and using primary data and sources, and accessing and interpreting a range of secondary sources.
Thinking, problem-solving, decision-making		Show deeper historical understanding, be more critical, think flexibly and make reasoned judgments.
Being creative		Demonstrate creativity and initiative when developing own ideas.
Working with others		Work effectively with others.
Self-management		Demonstrate self-management by working systematically, persisting with tasks, evaluating and improving own performance.

Key element	Description
Personal understanding	Explore how history has affected your identity, culture and lifestyle.
Mutual understanding	Investigate how history has been selectively interpreted to create stereotypical perceptions and to justify views and actions.
Personal health	Investigate how and why health standards have changed over time.
Moral character	Investigate individuals who are considered to have taken a significant moral stand and examine their motivation and legacy.
Spiritual awareness	Investigate and evaluate the spiritual beliefs and legacy of civilisations.
Citizenship	Investigate the long- and short-term causes and consequences of the partition of Ireland and how it has influenced Northern Ireland today, including key events and turning points.
Cultural understanding	Investigate the impact of significant events and ideas of the twentieth century on the world.
Media awareness	Critically investigate and evaluate the power of the media in their representation of a significant, historical event or individual.
Ethical awareness	Investigate ethical issues in history or historical figures who have behaved ethically or unethically.
Employability	Investigate how the skills developed through history will be useful in a range of careers, and the characteristics and achievements of entrepreneurs over time.
Economic awareness	Investigate the changing nature of local and global economies over time, and the impact of technology in the workplace over time.
Education for sustainable development	Investigate the need to preserve history in the local and global environment and evaluate the environmental impact of wars, industrial revolution, etc.

1 What is history?

In this chapter we are learning to:
- ✓ sort and classify evidence;
- ✓ compare and contrast different sources of information;
- ✓ reach conclusions based on evidence;
- ✓ identify the skills that studying history develops;
- ✓ create a spider diagram to show the important points we have learned about what history is.

If you enjoyed history in primary school, it was probably because you learned that history tells the story of people's lives in the past and what motivated them to change things. You may have liked asking questions about how people in the past lived, how they got themselves into trouble and how they got themselves out of it. In this chapter you will investigate what you think history is about.

GET ACTIVE 1

a Think about the statements the characters on the opposite page make about what history is. Which ones do you agree or disagree with?

b Write a list of the statements and rank them, with the one you agree with most at the top and the one you agree with least at the bottom.

c Compare your list with a partner. Is the order of the statements in your lists different? Discuss your reasons for your ranking and come up with a new list you both agree on.

d Share your ideas with the rest of the class and say which of the statements you feel best describes what history is about. Can you reach an agreement as a class on one statement that best describes history?

Have you ever wondered where the word 'history' comes from? It comes from the Greek word históreo *meaning 'to enquire about something'.*

History is about ENQUIRY, which for the historian means asking questions about the past so that we can make sense of it.

YOU ARE HISTORY!

Did you realise that history is all around you? It is in the buildings you see, the pop songs you listen to, the clothes you wear and the tools and TECHNOLOGY you use. Everything you see and use was first made in the past and all the things you think are good and bad are built on the ideas of people who came before you. Now you are adding to them and you are part of what people in the future will call 'history'. You are 'history'. You are connected to the past and to the future.

HISTORY IS ...

... asking questions about evidence.

... all about dates and facts.

... deciding who or what is important in the past and why.

... finding out about the past.

... working out reasons why things happened.

... using different sources of information.

... putting dates in the right order.

... writing down everything you know.

HOW DO HISTORIANS DO HISTORY?

Learning about the past and the methods used by historians to study the past will help you make sense of the world you live in. In the cartoons below you can see some of the skills historians use to carry out their investigations.

First, a historian gathers EVIDENCE. This evidence could both be primary (from the time) or secondary (produced after the time).

The historian then sorts the evidence – quite often they will do this in date order (chronologically).

The historian then begins to ask questions about the evidence so that he or she can check if it is reliable or not.

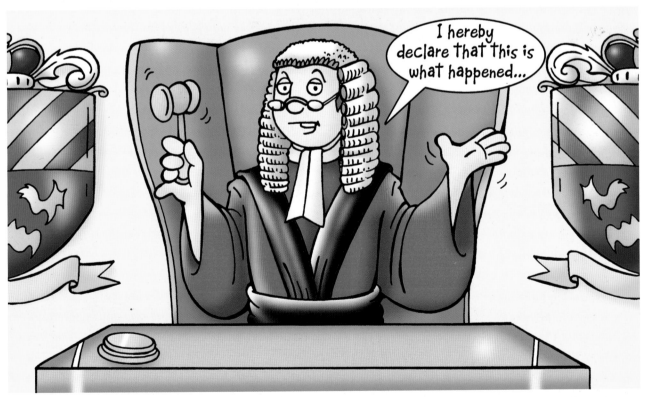

Finally, the historian tries to make sense of the evidence in order to make his or her own CONCLUSIONS about what happened in the past and why it happened.

GET ACTIVE 2

Gathering the evidence

a As we have seen, the first thing historians have to do is to gather evidence to answer some questions they may have about the past. On pages 6–7, six pieces of evidence have been gathered for you from different times in Irish history. With a partner, discuss why you think each of these images has been gathered. In your discussion, focus on what you can learn from each image about the history of Ireland and what clues in each picture help you to do this.

Sorting the evidence

b The next thing historians do is to sort their evidence. With your partner, try to sequence the pictures on pages 6–7 into CHRONOLOGICAL ORDER. Use the results from your discussion in part a) to help you to do this.

c Which clues did you use to put your evidence in order? For each picture, list the clues that helped you to make your decision.

d Are there some events shown in the pictures which you found hard to date? What further clues would you have needed to help you?

SORTING THE EVIDENCE

In Get Active 2 on page 6 you tried sorting the evidence by looking at the clues in the pictures alone. Further information which would have helped you is the captions to go alongside them. Below are the captions which go with the six pictures on pages 6–7.

a A drawing taken from an Orange Order flag showing Protestants being killed by Catholics in the 1641 rebellion in Ireland.

b A wall mural showing King William III at the Battle of the Boyne in 1690.

c A painting called *Men of the South* by Irish artist Sean Keating, dated 1920. It shows IRA flying columns during the War of Independence fought between English forces and the IRA, 1919–1921.

d A photo taken by a BBC reporter showing clashes between Catholics and the RUC in the Bogside region of Derry in 1969. This was known as 'The Battle of the Bogside'.

e A medieval sourcebook called *Expugnatio Hibernica: The Conquest of Ireland*, written by a Welsh churchman called Gerald of Wales in the twelfth century.

f A photo showing the Parliament buildings at Stormont after the Assembly had been dissolved in 2003. When published in the *Belfast Telegraph*, May 2005, it was captioned 'Dormant Stormont'.

GET ACTIVE 3

a Match the caption to each of the pictures on pages 6–7.

b Does having the captions change the chronological order in which you would put the pictures in Get Active 2? If so, re-order them so they are now in the correct chronological order.

c What does the work you have done in this chapter so far tell you about the limitations of just having the picture sources as evidence without any further information?

ASKING AND ANSWERING QUESTIONS

Even when evidence is sorted, it means very little unless it is used to answer the right questions. Historians ask questions such as 'who were the Normans?' or 'what happened to them?' They then make use of the evidence they have to see if it is useful in helping them answer their questions. This is called an enquiry.

GET ACTIVE 4

a With a partner, choose which of the six pictures on pages 6–7 you would use as pieces of evidence to help you answer the five questions in the Question Bank on page 9.

b Make up your own question and identify the picture you would choose to help answer it.

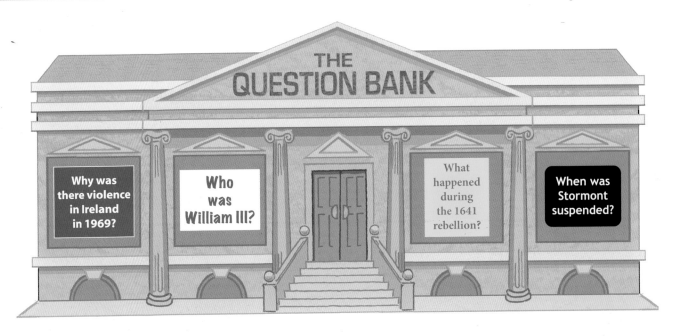

THE
QUESTION BANK

Why was there violence in Ireland in 1969?

Who was William III?

What happened during the 1641 rebellion?

When was Stormont suspended?

REACHING A CONCLUSION

As well as gathering and sorting evidence and asking and answering questions, historians have to come to conclusions about the pieces of evidence they are using in an enquiry.

a

I am certain that pictures 1–6 are all useful in showing me in what has happened in Irish history since the twelfth century.

c

b

Pictures 1–6 are probably useful to show aspects of what has happened in Irish history since the twelfth century but I need more evidence before I can be completely certain.

I am very unsure about pictures 1–6 being useful at all and I do not have any evidence to suggest an answer to the enquiry 'What has happened in Irish history since the twelfth century?'

GET ACTIVE 5

The three historians shown on the left have come to a conclusion about the evidence in pictures 1–6 (pages 6–7) which they have used in the enquiry: 'What has happened in Irish history since the twelfth century?'

a Choose the conclusion you most agree with and give reasons for your choice.

b Now make up your own concluding statement about the evidence in pictures 1–6, in terms of how well it helps you answer the same enquiry.

TAKING IT FURTHER – DOES HISTORY REALLY MATTER?

Is history a study of things that are dead and don't really matter? Can you learn anything in history that matters very much to your life? The historians' skills you have started to use in this chapter will help provide you with the skills employers are looking for, as well as helping you to have fun in your history class.

WILL DOING HISTORY GET ME A JOB?

GET ACTIVE 6

a Look at the illustration below. Can you match five of the statements about what the employers want to the five statements about what you have learned? Can you identify where in the chapter you used each of the skills in the statements?

b The employers also say they want problem solvers. Decide on what should go in the empty pupil speech bubble to show how you developed this skill. (Tip – think back to the work you did on gathering evidence.)

c What has this activity shown you about how studying history can be useful for other things too? Discuss your ideas with a partner.

SOURCE 1

BLOODY LESSON THAT WAS WELL LEARNED

We still remember the Somme as the senseless slaughter of men led by bungling generals. July 1, 1916 proved the most catastrophic day in the history of the British army. Of the 120,000 men who took part, 20,000 were dead and more than 40,000 wounded by nightfall. [...] 'Historians now see it as a turning point', said Mr Steel of the Imperial War Museum. 'The generals were quick to learn the lesson.'

The Times, Saturday 1 July 2006

IS HISTORY RELEVANT?

Newspapers and television news tell us what is going on in the world today. However, in order to help us understand current events better, news stories often need to draw information from the past. For example, July 2006 marked the ninetieth anniversary of the Battle of the Somme (one of the longest and bloodiest of the First World War) and commemoration services were held in Northern Ireland, the Republic of Ireland, Britain and Europe. The media reported on these commemorative events, and explained why they were taking place, by drawing on history (see Source 1).

When we read this news story in Source 1 we begin to understand why people today should remember the Somme, as well as the lessons that can be learned by future generations of generals and by ourselves. To look back at the background and origin of any event is called looking at its historical context.

CAN WE ALWAYS BELIEVE WHAT WE READ IN THE NEWS?

History also teaches you to be a critical thinker and not just accept things at face value. This is an important skill today in a world where we get a lot of different messages from the media. News stories can present the same facts in many different ways, and even news stories written on the same day and about the same event can present different viewpoints. The skills you will learn in history about questioning evidence will give you the opportunity to go beyond what you read and hear in the news and be critical, and also to ask questions and form your own opinions.

GET ACTIVE 7

The four headlines on page 13 are from different sources, but were all written on the same day, 11 July 2006. They report the same event – the sending off of the French captain Zinedine Zidane in the dying moments of the 2006 World Cup final. Read the headlines, then answer the following questions:

a Which headline gives you the best information about what may have happened?

b Which headline gives you a good reason why the incident happened?

c Which headline gives you the best information about who was involved?

d Why do you think newspapers have different viewpoints about the same event?

e Discuss what this activity has shown you about why it is important to be a critical thinker.

Zinedine Zidane (left, in white), Italian captain Cannavaro and Marco Materazzi (on the ground) seconds after the 'headbutting' at the World Cup final in Berlin on 9 July 2006.

Why ZZ blew his top!
Daily Mirror Northern Ireland

Zidane the flawed genius
BBC SPORT online

Can you believe it? With FIFA sadly yes
Belfast Telegraph SPORT

Agent: Materazzi provoked Zidane
Irish News, Tuesday

Sometimes in history we are presented with different viewpoints about the same event depending on the sources we use. The skills you used in this chapter – asking questions, comparing and contrasting different sources of information and recognising the limitations of some sources – are all very useful to help you develop the critical thinking skills you need not only to study history, but also to understand the world in which you live. These skills will be further developed throughout the rest of the course.

Plan, Do, Review

WHAT IS HISTORY?

In this chapter you looked at what history was about, then you worked through how historians do history, and finally you learned about what skills history can develop. You are now going to make a spider diagram called 'What is history?'

A spider diagram is a way of presenting in note form what you have learned. It has a title in the centre and each strand has a subtitle with words or phrases about important points you may want to remember.

PLAN

- First look at the subtitles on the strands on the spider diagram opposite.
- Then go back through your work in this chapter and highlight any words, phrases or sentences you think are important to help you make notes on the strands.

DO

- Now draw your own spider diagram with 'What is history?' as your central title and the other four titles written on the strands (as in the example opposite).
- Add further strands coming off these strands with the words, phrases or sentences you chose at the planning stage. You may wish to add images to help you remember the key points.

REVIEW

- Describe your spider diagram to a partner, explaining how you came to your decisions about what to put on it.
- Ask your partner if they think that you have missed anything important, and decide whether you need to add anything to your diagram.
- Now explain to the rest of the class:

  a three things you learned about what history is;
  b two things you found difficult about this chapter;
  c one question you still have about what history is.

2 Who am I?

In this chapter we are learning to:
- ✓ manage information to find out about our own personal history;
- ✓ place events in chronological order;
- ✓ recognise how the past has shaped identity in Northern Ireland;
- ✓ make a presentation about how the past has shaped us.

GET ACTIVE 1

What can you find out about Rory from the clues on his handprint?

WHAT'S IN A NAME?

Below is Rory Boomer Fitzgerald's handprint. His name gives us a clue about his identity and his past. In history, we are always looking for different clues about the past. These clues can be written, oral, visual or physical.

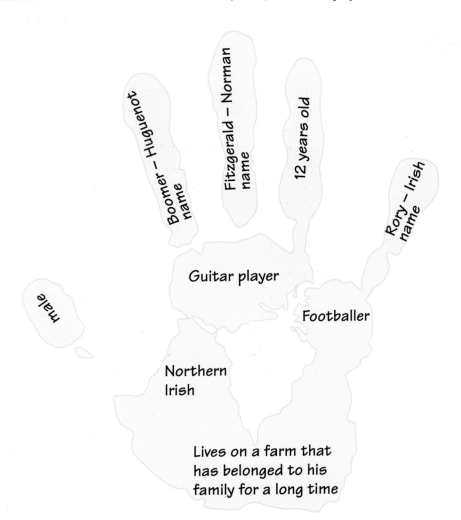

Boomer – Huguenot name

Fitzgerald – Norman name

12 years old

Rory – Irish name

Guitar player

male

Footballer

Northern Irish

Lives on a farm that has belonged to his family for a long time

HOW DOES THE PAST SHAPE ME?

Who we are today is influenced by what has happened before. By looking back into the past we can find out important things about ourselves. For example, where we were born, details about our family, and how we have changed over the years. Without the past we cannot understand who we really are. That is why studying history is so important. The past can shape our **IDENTITY** because it can help to explain our name, religion, **ETHNIC GROUP** and **NATIONALITY**. Look at the road map of Rory's past below.

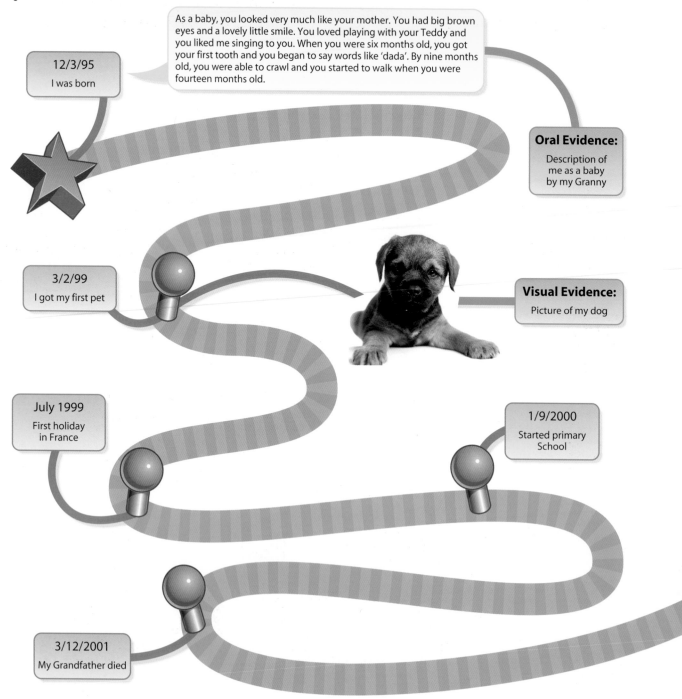

12/3/95
I was born

As a baby, you looked very much like your mother. You had big brown eyes and a lovely little smile. You loved playing with your Teddy and you liked me singing to you. When you were six months old, you got your first tooth and you began to say words like 'dada'. By nine months old, you were able to crawl and you started to walk when you were fourteen months old.

Oral Evidence:
Description of me as a baby by my Granny

3/2/99
I got my first pet

Visual Evidence:
Picture of my dog

July 1999
First holiday in France

1/9/2000
Started primary School

3/12/2001
My Grandfather died

GET ACTIVE 2

You are now going to place events from your own life in chronological order.

a Draw a road map of your life like Rory's shown below. On your map, place key events from when you were born until the present day. For each key event, think about the different sources of information you could use as evidence for the event. Try to think of:
- a visual piece of evidence – e.g. a photo;
- an oral piece of evidence – e.g. ask a relative information about yourself in the past;
- a written piece of evidence – e.g. a diary or a letter;
- a physical piece of evidence – e.g. something that belonged to you when you were younger.

b For homework, collect together one example of each type of evidence and add it to your road map (you could take a photo of your physical evidence).

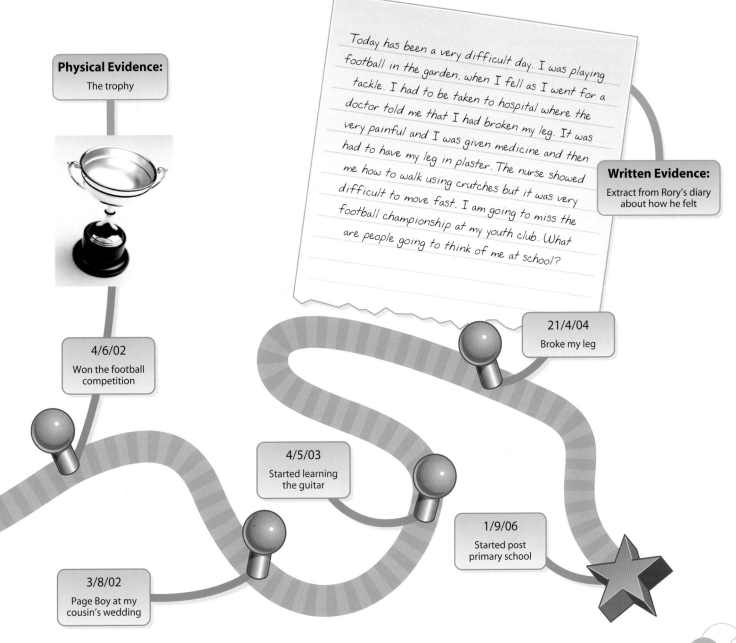

Physical Evidence:
The trophy

Today has been a very difficult day. I was playing football in the garden, when I fell as I went for a tackle. I had to be taken to hospital where the doctor told me that I had broken my leg. It was very painful and I was given medicine and then had to have my leg in plaster. The nurse showed me how to walk using crutches but it was very difficult to move fast. I am going to miss the football championship at my youth club. What are people going to think of me at school?

Written Evidence:
Extract from Rory's diary about how he felt

21/4/04
Broke my leg

4/6/02
Won the football competition

4/5/03
Started learning the guitar

1/9/06
Started post primary school

3/8/02
Page Boy at my cousin's wedding

HOW DO KEY EVENTS THROUGHOUT THE WORLD SHAPE ME?

In your road map from Get Active 2 (page 17) you identified personal events in the past which have helped shape who you are. However, when looking at the past, there are other layers of events – local, national, European and global – which have an influence on our lives.

It is important to recognise that events that happen around the world can affect our lives in Northern Ireland. For example:

On 11 September 2001, four planes where hijacked in the USA by members of a terrorist group. Two of the planes were flown into the World Trade Center towers in New York, as shown in the photo. As a result, we now have tighter security whenever we travel from Northern Ireland.

... and that local events in Northern Ireland can also affect life in other parts of the world. For example:

One of the first portable heart defibrillators in the world that jump-start the heart back to life after a heart attack. It was developed by Frank Pantridge in Northern Ireland and has been used around the world to save lives.

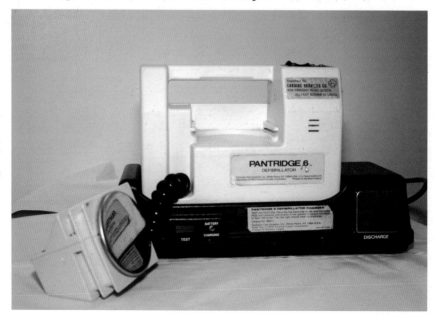

Always try to remember, when studying history, the importance of looking at these different layers to get a fuller understanding of what really happened in the past.

GET ACTIVE 3

In groups, you are now going to find out about key events which took place in Northern Ireland, Europe and the world during your lifetime. A key event is something that is considered to be more important than other events. Examples of key events are:

- the Good Friday Agreement in 1998;
- the Labour Party coming to power in the UK in 1997;
- Ireland adopting the Euro in 1999;
- Ulster winning the European Rugby Cup in 1999;
- the tsunami in south east Asia in 2004.

a In groups of four, number yourselves 1 to 4.
  - Number 1 needs to find out three key events that have taken place in Northern Ireland during your lifetime.
  - Number 2 needs to find out three key events that have taken place in Britain or Ireland during your lifetime.
  - Number 3 needs to find out three key events that have taken place in Europe during your lifetime.
  - Number 4 needs to find out three key events that have taken place in the world during your lifetime.

b Plan in your group how to carry out this task:
  - Where are you going to get your information?
  - How are you going to select the key events?
  - How are you going to present your key events visually?

c After you have found out your three key events, present them to your group. Each member of your group should present their events, so your group ends up with twelve key events in total.

d In your group, choose eight of the events which you think are most important.

e Prepare a visual diagram of your group's eight key events showing how they have affected your lives. Remember you can use words and pictures to present your information (for example as a road map, ripple chart, timeline or something else).

f As a group, present your diagram to the rest of the class. In your presentation, you should give reasons why you selected the eight events that you did and why you decided to leave out the others.

g Now return to your road map from Get Active 2 on page 17 – would you add to it any of the key events from your group work?

Good Friday Agreement, 1998

Ulster win Heineken Rugby Cup, 1999

Tsunami, South East Asia, 2004

GET ACTIVE 4

Use the timeline on pages 22–23 to check your answers to parts a) and b).

a List the people on pages 20–21 below in the correct chronological order according to when they came to Ireland.
b Add to your list the century in which they arrived.
c In what century were you born? Add yourself to the list.

HOW GOOD AM I AT CHRONOLOGY?

A timeline is a way to record events in history. Events need to be placed in the order in which they happen. As you learned in chapter 1, this is called chronological order. For example, your road map in Get Active 2, page 17, was a timeline.

Look at the timeline on pages 22–3. You will notice that some of the dates have AD before them or BC after them. When the timeline covers a long period of time, we have to think about adding BC and AD to the dates. BC refers to those events that took place before the birth of Christ, while AD refers to those events that took place after the birth of Christ. The letters AD stand for the Latin *anno domini*, which means 'in the year of our Lord'. We count the years BC backwards because every year that passed was nearer the birth of Christ. A century is a hundred years and a decade is ten years. The first century AD was from the birth of Christ to AD100.

a French Huguenot

b Mesolithic

c Chinese

d Norman

e Neolithic

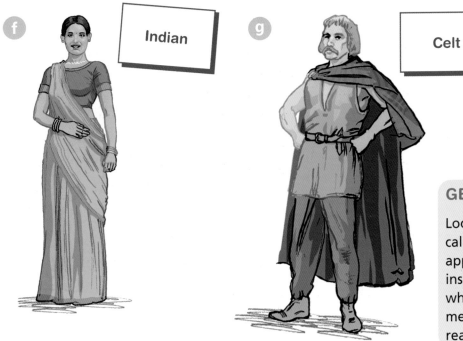

f Indian

g Celt

SPOTTING ANACHRONISMS

When looking at the past we have to be careful that we do not get time periods mixed up. On a timeline it is important that events are placed in the correct order. When something from one time period is placed in another we call this an ANACHRONISM.

0800 00 1066

HOW HAS THE PAST SHAPED OUR IDENTITY?

In this chapter you have looked at how certain events in your past have helped shape who you are and how key events throughout the world can also have an impact on life in Northern Ireland. Other factors that shape us are the different traditions, music, languages, sports and religions of the country we live in. These things have also been shaped by the country's past.

In the past, many different groups of people came to settle in Ireland. The timeline on pages 22–3 shows some of them. They came for different reasons. Here are three of them:

- economic – to earn more money, or have a better standard of living;
- political – to gain more power;
- religious – to escape persecution, or to spread their religion.

Mesolithic – 7000BC
Mesolithic people made their first settlements in Ireland close to rivers and lived off the food they hunted or gathered.

Neolithic – 3500BC
Neolithic people or first farmers came from Egypt and spread across Europe introducing farming methods. They had NOMADIC lifestyles and they came to Ireland to find land to farm. Music, stories and news were spread from place to place through travel.

Celts – 500BC
The Celts came from around the River Danube in central Europe, in search of land on which to settle. They brought Druidism to Ireland. The Celtic language was spoken across Ireland by AD400.

Jews – 1860s and 1880s
In the 1880s Jewish people came from eastern Europe to escape religious persecution. Many settled in North Belfast. They had jobs in the professions, trades and manufacturing.

Italians – 1800s
In the 1800s, the area around York Street in Belfast became known as 'little Italy' because of the high number of Italians who came to Belfast. Some set up cafés and ice cream shops. They came to Ireland to find a better life.

French Huguenots – 1685
These were French Protestants who came to Ireland when Protestantism was banned in France. A number of them settled in Co. Down and started the linen trade, making Ulster wealthier than other parts of Ireland.

Indians – 1920s and 1930s
Indian settlers from the Punjab and Gujarat regions of the sub-continent came to Northern Ireland to escape conflict in India and to set up businesses.

Chinese – 1960s
Chinese settlers came to Northern Ireland in the 1960s to escape economic hardship and to find work. The first Chinese restaurant in Northern Ireland opened in 1962.

Christians – AD432
Christianity came to Ireland with the arrival of St Patrick, who had been sent with the blessing of the Pope to bring Christianity to Ireland.

Vikings – AD700–800
The Vikings came to Ireland for land and trade. They introduced the use of coins to Ireland and formed settlements which still exist today.

Normans – AD1169
The Normans arrived in Ireland with the aid of the Irishman Dermot MacMurrough. They brought their own forms of farming, law, architecture, government and language to Ireland. Many names in Ireland today are of Norman origin, like Butler.

English and Scottish – 1600s
James I of England and VI of Scotland wanted to control Ireland more closely by giving Protestant settlers plantations. Towns like Coleraine and Londonderry were built for this reason. Many settlers were Protestant, and spread Protestantism in Ireland.

Vietnamese – 1970s
Vietnamese settlers in Northern Ireland were known as the 'boat people'. They had fled Vietnam for fear of persecution from the Communist forces who had taken over Vietnam after the end of the Vietnam War (1962–75).

Pakistanis – 1970s
People from Pakistan came to Britain to escape the political conflict and instability in Pakistan after its separation from India in 1947. In the 1970s, some Pakistanis left Britain and came to Northern Ireland in search of work.

Eastern Europeans – 2000s
With the enlargement of the European Union in 2004, people have come to Northern Ireland from eastern European countries such as Poland in order to work.

GET ACTIVE 7

a Design your own pot of stew like the one below – what peoples shaped your identity? You can add other nationalities not mentioned in this chapter.

b As a whole class, make a class stew to show all the different peoples that have shaped the identity of your class.

NORTHERN IRELAND TODAY

As we have seen, many different groups of people came to settle here in the past. Somebody who comes to a country from another region is called an **IMMIGRANT**. As a result of immigration, there are people in Northern Ireland who would identify themselves as British, Catholic, Chinese, Irish, Indian, Jewish, Nationalist, Protestant, Traveller, Unionist, European, Northern Irish and so on, or as a mixture of two nationalities such as Chinese-Irish.

The Northern Irish stew

What ingredients make up our society today? What peoples shaped our identity? Are we not all descendants of immigrants to Ireland?

As well as coming to Ireland, many people have also left Ireland over the centuries to go and live in other places. We call these people **EMIGRANTS**.

GET ACTIVE 8

Let's do some research.

a Has anyone in your family, or a friend of your family emigrated? Think about how you can find out this information. Who would you need to ask? If none of your family or friends of your family have emigrated, search the internet to find someone who emigrated from Ireland.

b For your chosen emigrant, try to find out the answers to the following questions:
  • Where did they go?
  • When did they go?
  • Why did they go?
  • What did they experience?
  • What other things would you like to find out?

c Share the information you have found out with the rest of the class.

Plan, Do, Review

WHO AM I?

In this chapter you have been finding out about how the past shapes who we are today. You are now going to prepare a two-minute presentation about how the past has shaped who you are. Your visual aid for the presentation could be your own handprint or footprint, like Rory's at the start of the chapter on page 15 or your own idea. This could include information about your name, where you are from, how people see you and events in your life.

PLAN

Stage 1 – Get your thoughts together

- Skim back through this chapter.
- Re-read the road map you made for yourself.
- What can you find out about your own name? Who were you named after or what does your name mean? What are the origins of your name? You may want to use books or the internet to find out about your name.
- Think about your identity. How would you describe yourself? How do others see you? What are the important things in your life that have shaped who you are? Can you connect with any of the peoples who came to Ireland?

Stage 2 – Plan your presentation

Having completed all your research you are now ready to plan your presentation.

- Decide on the visual aid for your presentation. Will it be a handprint, footprint or your own idea?
- Decide what information you are going to select to be presented.

- Decide on the most interesting way to present your information. Will you use words, pictures or even actual physical pieces of evidence?
- Plan carefully what you are going to say and how you are going to say it. How will you keep the interest of your audience? Practise your presentation aloud and plan how it will end.

DO

- Make your presentation to the rest of the class.
- Keep to your time limit of no more than two minutes for the presentation.

REVIEW

- What two things did you do well? Record these in two stars like the ones below.
- What would you like to do better? Record this as a wish in a thought cloud like the one below.

3 Why did the Normans invade Ireland in 1169?

In this chapter we are learning to:
- ✓ research independently to find out why the Normans invaded England;
- ✓ identify the reasons why the Normans came to Ireland in 1169;
- ✓ sort and prioritise the reasons to explain why the Normans came to Ireland;
- ✓ be creative in designing a website about why the Normans invaded Ireland.

WHO WERE THE NORMANS?

It is important that we find out about the Normans because they left many things which have shaped life today. Across Northern Ireland you can see mounds of earth such as the one shown in the picture below. These mounds of earth were once an early form of castle and were called 'motte and bailey' castles. You can also see castles such as the one at Carrickfergus shown on the front cover of this book. Have you ever wondered who built these and why? They were built by people known as the Normans. They came from Normandy and invaded England in 1066.

Motte and bailey castle in Clough, built either during or before the reign of King John (1189–1216)

GET ACTIVE 1

What can you find out about the Normans and how they invaded England in 1066?

a Decide on five questions that you would like to ask, and find the answers using books or the internet. For example:
- • Who were the Normans?
- • Why did they want to come to England?
- • How did they come to England?
- • Exactly when did they come to England?
- • What were the results of them coming to England?

b Choose the format in which to present your information, for example a pamphlet, a fact file, a flier or a word-processed report. You could insert graphics to help you illustrate the answers to your questions.

WHAT DO PEOPLE THINK ABOUT THE NORMANS?

In 1169 the Normans decided to invade Ireland. Today Northern Ireland is part of the United Kingdom, and the reason it is can be traced back to the invasion of the Normans in 1169. Some people think the arrival of the Normans was a good thing for Ireland, because it brought new systems of farming, law, architecture and culture. Others think the arrival of the Normans was a bad thing, because the people of Ireland were ruled by foreigners and some of the Irish ways of life were replaced with Norman ones. What do you think?

GET ACTIVE 2

a Use Source 1 to decide if the statement 'The Normans and the Irish were good friends' is true or false. Remember to explain your answer.

b When using sources of information, we need to be careful about basing our opinions on just one source. Now read Source 2. Use Source 2 to decide if the statement 'The Normans and the Irish were good friends' is true or false or neither.

c What different viewpoints can you see in Sources 3 and 4? Complete the following sentences:
  • Source 3 gives the viewpoint that the arrival of the Normans in Ireland was …
  • The viewpoint in Source 4 sees the arrival of the Normans in Ireland as …

d Make a list of all the things the Normans brought to Ireland mentioned in Source 4. Which one do you think is the most important? Which one do you think is the least important? Give reasons for you answer.

SOURCE 1

We have a natural hostility to each other arising from the slaying of fathers, brothers, nephews and other near relatives and friends on both sides so that we have no desire for friendship.

Adapted from a letter from the Irish chieftain Donal O'Neill to the Pope explaining the hostility between the Irish and the Normans in 1317

SOURCE 2

At the CONQUEST of Ireland, the Normans used the English language, dress and ways of riding a horse. But now many Norman English have adopted the manners, fashion and language of the Irish. They have married and made ALLIANCES with the Irish.

Adapted from the first part of the Statutes of Kilkenny written in 1366.

SOURCE 3

In 1170, at the request of the King of Leinster, Richard Fitzgilbert de Clare, the Earl of Pembroke (also known as 'Strongbow') led a Norman army from England into Ireland. The Normans swiftly conquered the island, which came under the domination of the English kings. Ireland spent the next 700 years under English rule (or misrule, as often was the case). Thereafter, almost every generation of Irish tried to rise against the foreign overlords. These uprisings were brutally crushed, Irish lands were given to lords in England and the Irish people starved and were beaten into submission.'

From a website on the Irish struggle for independence, 1916–23

SOURCE 4

English was first written and spoken in Ireland by the Normans. The Normans were the first to hold parliaments in Ireland and it was they who first brought the island under the control of the English Crown. Our speech, our law, our system of government, our political divisions; all can be seen to be the LEGACY of the Normans. You can still see the remains of over 2000 castles built by the Normans. They founded many important towns such as Coleraine, Carrickfergus, Dundalk, Drogheda, Kilkenny, Tralee, Galway, Sligo and Clonmel. The Normans left us a varied and important legacy.

Written by Brendan Smith in 1993 in Ireland and the Normans: Progress or Decline?

You have been looking at who the Normans were and how people viewed them in the past and how they are viewed today. It is now important to find out how and why they came to Ireland in 1169. Before the Normans came, Ireland was divided into different kingdoms with one High King. You are now going to read the story of Dermot MacMurrough and his role in bringing the Normans to Ireland.

The Story of Dermot and Dervorgilla

Dermot had a sad childhood. When he was five, his father was murdered by the men of Dublin. He became King of Leinster when he was only sixteen. This was a violent time to live in Ireland. Many of the kings fought each other for power. Dermot lived in fear of his life, as his enemies could take any opportunity to kill him.

One way to gain powerful friends was to marry the daughter of a king. So Dermot married Mor O'Toole, the daughter of the King of Uí Muireadhaigh, whose brother Laurence O'Toole became Archbishop of Dublin. Dermot and Mor had six children.

One day, Dermot met Dervorgilla, wife of Tiernan O'Rourke, the King of Briefne. They fell in love and started to send each other love letters. Dervorgilla wanted to be with Dermot so much that one day, in 1152, she sent him a letter telling him that her husband Tiernan was away on a pilgrimage. Dermot and Tiernan O'Rourke were enemies.

Dermot got his men together and went to O'Rourke's stronghold and seized Dervorgilla. They brought her cattle and furniture with them to Dermot's stronghold at Ferns. Dermot and Dervorgilla were now together.

Tiernan was very angry when he returned from his pilgrimage. He began to plan his revenge.

He decided to go to Turlough O'Connor, the High King, to get help. In 1153, the High King led men to Ferns and captured Dervorgilla, returning her to her husband, Tiernan. The love story between Dervorgilla and Dermot was over.

Tiernan remained bitter and angry with Dermot. In 1166, Tiernan got his chance to get even with Dermot. There was a new High King called Rory, who was Turlough's son. Rory did not trust Dermot and he wanted Leinster, Dermot's kingdom, to be ruled by one of his friends. So Rory joined with Tiernan and the King of Meath to march to Leinster and drive Dermot out of his lands. On 1 August 1166, Dermot was forced to leave Ireland. He was devastated. He had lost his love and now all his lands as well. Who could he turn to? His only option was to go and get help from the Normans in Wales, with whom he had traded goods. All that mattered to him was that he could return to his land and drive out his enemies O'Rourke and O'Connor. What could he promise the Normans in return?…

GET ACTIVE 3

You are going to decide on the key points in this story of Dermot and Dervorgilla to understand why he had to turn to the Normans to help him regain his lands in Ireland. Then, in Get Active 4, you will do a role play of the story.

a Get into pairs. Take it in turns to read the story aloud to each other.

b Individually, write down key words, phrases, dates and events.

c Compare your list with your partner's. Decide on the most important key words, phrases, dates and events.

d Share these with another pair and, as a group of four, decide on the most important and make a group list of the key words, phrases, dates and events.

e Share your group's list with the class and agree on a class list.

GET ACTIVE 4

a In groups, prepare a role play of the story of Dermot and Dervorgilla, making sure you cover all the key words, phrases, dates and events on your class list from Get Active 3. You can prepare your role play by creating a storyboard. Filmmakers create storyboards before they start filming to decide the content of each scene. You will need to decide how many scenes your role play will have and then create a storyboard to show their content. You can show the content of the scenes using pictures, words and phrases.

b Now, using your storyboard, rehearse your role play and then act it out to the rest of the class.

WHAT REALLY HAPPENED IN 1152?

The story of Dermot and Dervorgilla on pages 28–9 is just one version of the events. There are other accounts of what happened which need investigating …

GET ACTIVE 5

Read the three different accounts of the story of Dermot and Dervorgilla.

a In your own words, explain the three different accounts of why Dervorgilla went to Ferns.

b Why are the stories different? Think about who wrote them.

c Which account do you think is most trustworthy? Give reasons for your answer.

d Why is it important to read more than one account of an event?

e What is Gerald of Wales' opinion in Account 1? Do you agree with his opinion? In what ways is this an example of a STEREOTYPE?

What happened in 1152?

ACCOUNT 1: ABDUCTION

The *Annals of Clonmacnoise* record that Dervorgilla was abducted by Dermot. It is important to note that these annals were written by monks who supported Tiernan O'Rourke. He did not want to be embarrassed by a story that would show that his wife left him for another man. Dermot was his enemy and he wanted an account that would show Dermot in a bad light.

Gerald of Wales, a clergyman of Norman and Welsh background, states: 'No doubt she was abducted because she wanted to be, and since most women are fickle she arranged for herself to be the kidnapper's prize. Almost all the world's most notable catastrophes have been caused by women – think of Cleopatra causing the death of Mark Antony and Helen of Troy and the destruction of Troy.'

ACCOUNT 2: PROTECTION

According to the *Annals of the Four Masters*, written by Irish monks in 1636, Dervorgilla, wife of Tiernan O'Rourke, was taken away by Dermot MacMurrough, King of Leinster, with her cattle and her furniture because Dervorgilla's brother had asked Dermot to keep her safe.

Brother Michael O' Clerigh writes in the *Annals of the Kingdom of Ireland* by the Four Masters in 1636 that 'a careful sifting of the evidence proves that there was no elopement and no romance. Dervorgilla, in our judgement, was taken away for safety with the consent of her family.'

ACCOUNT 3: ELOPEMENT

The *Song of Dermot and the Earl*, written by a Norman who served Dermot, shows that Dervorgilla loved Dermot and she arranged the elopement. The poem says:

That she would let King Dermot know
In what place he should take her
Where she should be in concealment

Editor's comment – think about it!

Dervorgilla died at Mellifont Abbey when she was 85 years old, on 25 January 1193. If she had eloped, she would have been considered breaking the law of marriage and nobody of noble rank would have associated with her. In 1157, five years after the event at Ferns, Dervorgilla attended the consecration of the first Cistercian monastery in Ireland. She presented gifts of gold in the presence of the High King and other noble people.

WHY DID THE NORMANS COME TO IRELAND?

As you learned in chapter 1, historians, like detectives, carry out enquiries to find out about the past. An enquiry is an investigation into what happened in the past and why it happened. It is important that at the end of an enquiry a conclusion is reached, based on the evidence that has been gathered. We are now going to carry out an enquiry to come to a conclusion about why the Normans came to Ireland. We have so far looked at a story about the role of Dermot MacMurrough. Now we are going to look at his role alongside some other evidence to see if there were other reasons why the Normans came to Ireland.

Dermot MacMurrough

I need to find soldiers to help me regain my lands in Leinster.

When Dermot arrived in Wales after he was forced to leave Ireland, he got permission from Henry II, King of England, to hire soldiers in England to take with him to Ireland to regain his lands. Four forces of Normans arrived in Ireland in May 1169, August 1169, May 1170 and August 1170. Henry II then came to Ireland in 1171.

Strongbow, Richard de Clare, Earl of Pembroke

Richard de Clare, Earl of Pembroke, also known as 'Strongbow', had angered Henry II by supporting one of his enemies, and as a result lost his lands and his title in England. Strongbow was eager to help Dermot in exchange for Dermot's daughter Aoife's hand in marriage as well as the promise of inheriting the lands of Leinster whenever Dermot died.

Here is the opportunity for me to gain land in Ireland and become a powerful lord by marrying Dermot MacMurrough's daughter.

I was imprisoned by a Welsh prince in 1167. The prince has agreed that I will re-gain my freedom and land if I invade Ireland with Dermot.

I have been promised land by Dermot and coming to Ireland will be a great adventure.

Robert Fitzstephen and Maurice Fitzgerald

The individual Normans who brought forces to Ireland realised that they could gain land in Ireland if they were successful in battle. Each Norman lord had their own personal reasons for coming to Ireland.

Pope Adrian IV

The Church in Ireland was strong, but it was not under the control of the Pope. In 1155, Pope Adrian IV issued a Papal Bull called *Laudabiliter*. This encouraged Henry II to invade Ireland so that the Irish Church and people could be reformed and come under the control of the Pope.

Bishop Adrian sends greeting to the King of the English … As a good Catholic prince, enter Ireland to declare the truth of the Christian faith to that barbarous nation. Make sure the people obey the laws of the Church so that the evil there can be removed. You, of course, will pay an annual pension to the Church in Rome.

Adapted from the Papal Bull Laudabiliter*, 1155*

I do not want any Norman lord becoming too powerful in Ireland. I have heard that when Dermot died in 1171, Strongbow became King of Leinster. Nobody becomes King in Ireland except me. It is time these Norman lords knew who is boss!

Henry II, King of England

Henry sailed for Ireland in October 1171. 'Strongbow' surrendered his lands in Ireland to Henry and swore him an OATH OF ALLEGIANCE. In return, Henry allowed him to be Lord of Leinster, but Dublin, Waterford and Wexford became property of the Crown. The Irish kings swore their allegiance to Henry as King, and the Treaty of Windsor (see page 40) was signed between the High King of Ireland Rory O'Connor and Henry II in 1175.

Plan, Do, Review

WHY DID THE NORMANS INVADE IRELAND IN 1169?

In this chapter you have found out about why the Normans came to England and Ireland. You have identified the different reasons why the Normans came to Ireland. Your task is to design a website giving information about why the Normans came to Ireland in 1169.

PLAN

When you design a website you have to plan it carefully. A website has a homepage and a number of link pages. Decide on the information that each page will contain. Here are some suggestions:

Homepage

Your homepage should introduce the Normans and who they were. It should have high visual impact and be inviting to people who want to explore your site. Re-read your report from Get Active 1, page 26, on why the Normans invaded England in 1066 and use any useful facts you researched.

Decide on what links your homepage should have. For example it could have links to:

- The Role of Dermot MacMurrough;
- The Role of Strongbow;
- The Role of Henry II;
- The Role of Pope Adrian IV.

An example of a homepage is given opposite.

Link pages

These pages could:

- Describe the role of Dermot MacMurrough in bringing the Normans to Ireland. Why did he need the Normans to help him? What did he promise them?
- Show why people like Strongbow, Fitzstephen and Fitzgerald came to Ireland. What did they have to gain?
- Examine the role of Henry II. How would invading strengthen his kingdom?
- Explain why Pope Adrian IV supported the Normans coming to Ireland. What did he want them to achieve?

DO

- Design the layout of the website. You need to decide on its background, the font size and any graphics that are to be included. Make sure that you include an icon on each link page which allows you to get back to the homepage.
- Now add the information to the homepage and link pages you have planned to include.

REVIEW

When you have completed your website, you can review your learning by completing the review triangle on the right.

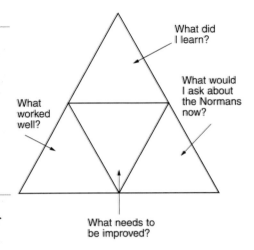

Think of what you need to ask yourself...

This is what your homepage could look like!

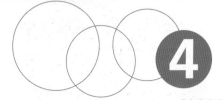

4 What were people in the past really like?

In this chapter we are learning to:
- ✓ investigate how individuals have made a difference in the past;
- ✓ appreciate that people can have different views and ideas about the past;
- ✓ be creative about reconstructing the past.

WHAT WAS DERMOT REALLY LIKE?

Dermot MacMurrough is one of the most controversial people in Irish history. People have different ideas about what he was like and what he did. Some people consider him a military and political hero. Others think that he was an evil and brutal man. He is also viewed as a holy man who built churches and helped spread Christianity. Some people regard him as a traitor because he invited the Normans into Ireland and so claim he is responsible for bringing the English into Ireland. Dermot lived almost 900 years ago, yet he is still remembered. This shows us that what you say and do can be remembered for a long time. What reputation does Dermot deserve?

GET ACTIVE 1

Think about people who are in the public eye today – politicians, musicians, actors – and ordinary people in your community. Does everyone have the same view of them? One of the ways we can find out what people are really like is to look at the evidence.

a Choose one person everyone knows about.
b Survey the members of your class to see if everyone has the same view of this person.
c What do people base their views on? Are their views based on evidence? Can you believe what you hear? Or what you read? Or what you see?

GET ACTIVE 2

To get an impression of what Dermot was like, re-read the story of Dermot and Dervorgilla on pages 28–9.

a What impression does the story give you of Dermot? In small groups, brainstorm the qualities or characteristics you think Dermot had.
b In your groups, discuss whether you can rely on the story as a piece of evidence. What would help you decide whether it gave a true impression of Dermot or not?

One thing that might help you decide is whether other sources of evidence support the impression of Dermot that the story gives. So, in order to judge what Dermot was really like, we need to look at several pieces of evidence.

Dermot MacMurrough, King of Leinster, who had spread terror throughout Ireland, after putting the English in possession of the country, committing excessive evils against the Irish people, and plundering and burning many churches … died this year of disease. He became putrid while living.

The Annals of the Four Masters, written by Irish monks in 1171

SOURCE 2

It is really a great miracle in our opinion that a King at the end of the Earth, ruling over barbarous peoples should undertake works of mercy and great generosity.

St Bernard, head of the Cistercian order of monks in France, writing to Dermot in 1148

SOURCE 3

See how the enemy of his country, that despot over his own people and universal enemy, previously driven from his country, has now returned flanked by the arms of foreigners, to bring about our common ruin.

A speech made by Rory O'Connor in 1170, quoted by Gerald of Wales, a clergyman of Norman and Welsh background in Expugnatio Hibernica: The Conquest of Ireland, *written in 1189*

GET ACTIVE 3

a Read Sources 1–4. What good points and what bad points do they make about Dermot? Copy and complete the table below to help you organise the evidence.

Source	Good Points	Bad Points
Source 1		
Source 2		
Source 3		
Source 4		

b Use the table you have completed to explain how Sources 1 and 2 differ in what they say about Dermot.

c Now add to your explanation, by saying why you think Sources 1 and 2 differ. To help you answer this, think about when the source was written, who wrote it and why.

d Now you have considered the evidence, re-visit your answer to Get Active 2a.
  • Has your examination of the evidence changed your mind about what Dermot was really like?
  • Has it helped you decide what type of reputation Dermot deserves?

SOURCE 4

Two hundred heads of his enemies were laid at Dermot's feet. He lifted up to his mouth the head of one he particularly loathed and taking it by the ears and hair, gnawed at the nose and cheeks – a cruel and most inhuman act.

From Expugnatio Hibernica: The Conquest of Ireland *by Gerald of Wales, written in 1189*

WHAT WAS LAURENCE O'TOOLE REALLY LIKE?

Laurence O'Toole lived at the same time as Dermot MacMurrough but had a very different reputation. He was well known for his work with the poor and his efforts to encourage people to live in a non-violent way. In Source 1 below, Laurence is shown giving bread to the poor.

GET ACTIVE 4

a What does the icon shown in Source 1 reveal about Laurence O'Toole? Make a list of the things it shows.

b Can Source 1 be believed as a true picture of what Laurence O'Toole was like? Give reasons.

c What else might you need to do to get an accurate idea of what Laurence was like?

SOURCE 1

Laurence's early life – he was cruelly treated by Dermot MacMurrough

Laurence at prayer

Bishop's mitre and robe, with a monk's habit worn underneath

The poor of Dublin, who Laurence cared for

Bare feet – a sign of humility

Glendalough, where Laurence was a monk

Christ Church Cathedral – Laurence is credited with building the crypt there

GET ACTIVE 5

a Study the statements made about Laurence and sort them into positive, negative and factual.
b What do these statements reveal about the kind of person Laurence was?

a Every day, Laurence invited the poor into his home where he gave them food.

b Ireland's economy was doing very well, but there was also a lot of poverty in Dublin.

c In 1175, Laurence played an important role in negotiating the Treaty of Windsor (see page 40) between Ireland's High King Rory O'Connor and the King of England, Henry II.

d Laurence was the brother of Dermot's wife, Mor.

e In September 1170, Laurence met Strongbow to discuss making peace with the Normans.

f Laurence was appointed Archbishop of Dublin in 1162.

g Laurence set up care centres for children who had been abandoned by their parents or who were orphaned in the city.

h Laurence saved many lives during the Norman raids on Dublin in 1170.

i Laurence was a MEDIATOR – he encouraged enemies to talk rather than use violence. He had a reputation as a peacemaker.

GET ACTIVE 6

Laurence and Dermot had very different lives and both made an impact on other people.

a What impact do you think each man made? Think of a long-term and a short-term impact for each of them.
b Which of these two historical figures do you admire most? Explain why.
c What kind of impact would you like to have on other people? How could you achieve this, both in the short and the long term?

WHO WAS JOHN DE COURCY?

The Treaty of Windsor of 1175 stated that Rory O'Connor would remain High King of Ireland in return for paying TRIBUTE to Henry II. Yet despite this, Norman knights continued to conquer Irish TERRITORY. One knight who claimed a lot of territory was John de Courcy. This is his story …

1

In 1177, the Norman knight John de Courcy marched from Dublin towards the North with 22 knights and about 300 soldiers.

2

The local king Rory MacDunleavy fled, but he returned a week later with a large army.

3

The Normans, with their bows and arrows, swords, armour and horses, had superior military strength and were able to defeat Rory and the Irish.

4

Downpatrick

John conquered most of Co. Antrim and Co. Down and gave himself the title of *Princeps Ultoniae*, which means 'Master of Ulster'.

5

John immediately began building castles to strengthen his control.

6

In 1180, John married Affreca, the daughter of Gottred, the Norse King of the Isle of Man. Gottred was a powerful king. The marriage meant John's kingdom would not be raided by the Vikings.

7

John built a castle and re-built the cathedral in Downpatrick, Rory MacDunleavy's former stronghold. John declared that the bones of St Patrick were found there.

8

John made coins with St Patrick's head on one side and his own head on the other. This angered Prince John of England.

9

In 1189, Henry II died and Prince John became King of England. King John now felt that John de Courcy was a threat to his power.

10

In 1204, King John ordered Hugh de Lacy, the ruler of Meath, to invade Ulster and overthrow John de Courcy. After a short war, John fled and spent the rest of his life in poverty in Europe.

GET ACTIVE 7

Stories from the past often make very good films.

a Draw up a list of well-known films that are set in the past.
b Use your list to brainstorm the elements you think make a successful historical film. Do any of the elements you have come up with appear in the story of John de Courcy?
c A successful film needs a good screenplay. This contains the action (what we see happening) and the dialogue (what the characters say). Look at the cartoon story of John again. Choose one scene in which he is with other people. Re-write that part of the story as a screenplay. You will need to write the dialogue and the instructions for the action.

11

As a reward, King John gave Hugh de Lacy all of John de Courcy's land and the title of Earl of Ulster.

CAN YOU BELIEVE EVERYTHING YOU READ?

Throughout this chapter we have started to question whether sources and evidence are reliable and to think about whether we can believe everything we read or hear. When you are looking at sources, there is a method you can use to check how reliable the evidence is. This is called the 'W5' method and is illustrated below (you already came across this on page 5). Remember, all evidence is useful – it depends on what you want to use it for – but not all is necessarily reliable. The 'W5' method will also help you to decide whether the evidence is useful for the enquiry you are carrying out.

Who? Who wrote the source? Did they have any beliefs or attitudes that might affect their views?

Why? Why was the source written? Did the author have a specific aim?

When? When was the source created? Did the writer have first-hand experience of the person or event they are writing about?

What? What information does the source give? Is it only fact or are opinions being given as well?

Where? Where was the source created?

Now let's use the 'W5' method to explore what John de Courcy was really like. Source 1 was created by Gerald of Wales. Gerald was a clergyman of Norman and Welsh background. In 1184, he was chosen to travel through Ireland with Prince John. He published his findings in 1189. In Source 1, he describes John de Courcy.

John was a tall, blond man with long bony limbs. He was physically very strong, and of exceptional courage. From his youth he had shown himself to be a valiant man of war, always first into action, always grasping the nettle in danger. In battle, he fought like a reckless common soldier rather than a careful commander, conscious of his value to his own troops. Yet, in ordinary life, he was a moderate and sober-minded man, who showed true reverence to Christ and his Church. He was utterly dedicated to the worship of his God and ready always to give God glory, when he had achieved any success.

Gerald of Wales, between 1184 and 1189

Applying the 'W5' method to Source 1 might look something like this.

Source 1	
Who?	Gerald of Wales – Norman/ Welsh clergyman. He might be on John's side.
What?	John was a strong man. He was courageous. He was very religious and believed God was responsible for his success.
Why?	Gerald was recording events in Ireland for Prince John.
When?	Sometime between 1184 and 1189
Where?	Ireland

GET ACTIVE 8

a In groups, apply the 'W5' method to Sources 2–5 in order to gather as much information about John as you can. Record your findings in a table like the one above.

b Then create a report sheet like the one below, using all the sources (1–5). You could add more questions if you want.

Investigation report	
Questions	**Answer 'yes', 'no' or 'not sure'. Include the number of the source which shows you this and any comments you feel you need to add.**
Was John a good soldier?	
Was John a very religious man?	
Was John a clever man?	

SOURCE 2

A white knight, astride a white horse, bearing a device of birds on his shield, will be the first to enter Ulaid and overrun it with hostile intent.

Prophecy by Merlin of Celidon, quoted by Gerald of Wales in 1189. Merlin 'the Magician' attended the court of King Arthur nearly 600 years before Gerald of Wales wrote his books. Merlin allegedly had supernatural powers and could predict the future.

SOURCE 3

In 1178, John de Courcy with his mercenaries committed terrible crimes, but Rory MacDunleavy, King of Ulaid, made a hostile attack upon them, drowning and otherwise killing 450 of them. One hundred of the Irish fell in battle. John de Courcy was not defeated, and soon after proceeded to plunder Ulaid.

The Annals of the Four Masters, 1178. Author unknown. The Annals were compiled between 1632 and 1636 by Michael O'Clery, a Franciscan monk. The entries for the twelfth century and before were sourced from medieval monastic annals.

SOURCE 4

John soon after proceeded to plunder Dalriada. He escaped with difficulty, being severely wounded, and he fled to Dublin.

The Annals of the Four Masters, 1178

SOURCE 5

Sir Hugh de Lacy was ordered to capture John de Courcy. He asked John's own men how this might be done. They said it was impossible, except on Good Friday when he would wear no shield, have no weapons, and would be praying in the church, barefoot. They attacked him, but he defended himself with the cross pole until it was broken and killed thirteen of his attackers before he was captured.

From the Book of Howth, a monastic annal, date unknown

SO WHAT WAS JOHN DE COURCY REALLY LIKE?

As you have seen, John is remembered for many things and people have differing views about him and the type of person he was. **INTERPRETATIONS** should be based on evidence, but sometimes opinions are presented as facts rather than points of view.

GET ACTIVE 9

a The boxes below contain both facts and opinions. Can you tell the difference? Create two lists – one for facts and one for opinions.

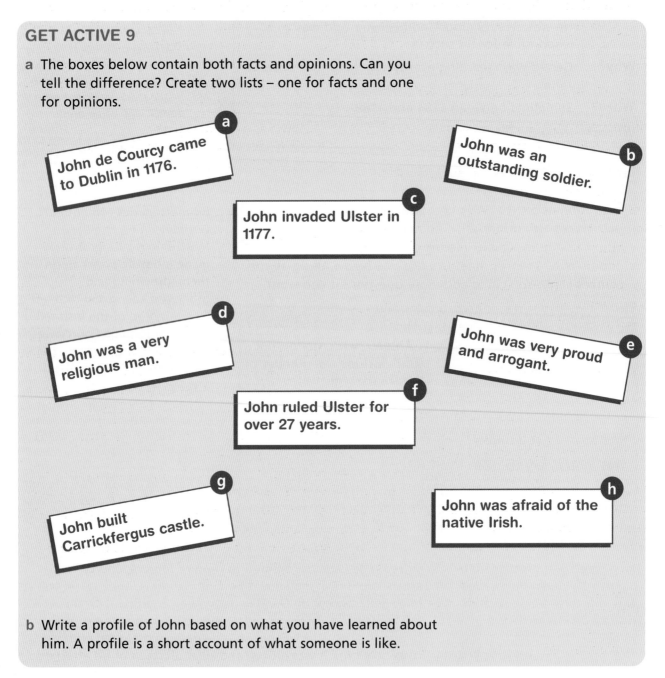

a John de Courcy came to Dublin in 1176.

b John was an outstanding soldier.

c John invaded Ulster in 1177.

d John was a very religious man.

e John was very proud and arrogant.

f John ruled Ulster for over 27 years.

g John built Carrickfergus castle.

h John was afraid of the native Irish.

b Write a profile of John based on what you have learned about him. A profile is a short account of what someone is like.

Plan, Do, Review

WHAT WERE PEOPLE IN THE PAST REALLY LIKE?

In this chapter, we have been trying to answer this question by looking at stories of people who lived over 800 years ago. To help us do this, we have thought about these issues along the way:

- People have different views and interpretations.
- It's important to reach balanced judgements, based on the evidence.

Your task is to write a short memoir of one of the characters you found out about in this chapter. This means that you will have to imagine you are that person. Your account must include both fact and opinion. You must include some of the information you read in the chapter but, because this is an imaginative piece, you can include some of your own ideas to fill in the gaps.

PLAN

Stage 1 – Decide on your character
Skim through the chapter again. Which of the characters did you find most interesting? Decide on the character you will write about.

Stage 2 – Decide on your style
What genre or type of memoir do you want to write? You could do a diary, a poem, even some rap lyrics. Do you want it to be:

- factual?
- exciting?
- interesting?
- gruesome?
- adventurous?

Stage 3 – Organise your ideas
Go back over the chapter and pick out key information about your character. Think about aspects that they would like to emphasise in their memoir. Brainstorm some useful verbs and adjectives. Decide how you are going to structure your work.

- How will you introduce it?
- What will be the focus in the middle part?
- How will you finish it off?

DO

Write your memoir. Remember to keep it interesting and to write as if you are the person you have chosen.

REVIEW

Once you have written your initial draft, check it over (someone else might help you with this) and see if you can improve it. Your work will be judged on whether you have:

- included some of the factual information from this chapter;
- incorporated some of your own ideas;
- given a particular point of view;
- convinced the reader that you really are the character;
- used vivid and exciting words to describe your life.

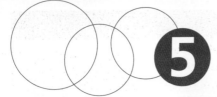

⑤ How did life in Ireland change during 1169–1500?

In this chapter we are learning to:
- ✓ make judgements about life in the past;
- ✓ understand continuity and change;
- ✓ work with others to represent ideas about how Ireland changed in a variety of ways.

GET ACTIVE 1

The table on page 47 shows the changes that took place in Ireland between 1169 and 1500. Your task is to begin creating a concept map to represent this information. Start your map in the same way as the one shown below and add any additional information you can get from the table. Leave enough space to add to your map as you work through this chapter.

The years between 1169 and 1500 were a time of great change in Ireland. They are often called the MEDIEVAL period, or the MIDDLE AGES.

- The Gaelic kings or chieftains were replaced by government from England.
- Ireland's population became more diverse, as Anglo-Norman settlers joined the native Celtic peoples and Viking invaders.
- The way people lived, worked, dressed and thought changed.
- Developments in techology meant Ireland became more connected to the outside world.

This was an exciting time to live in, and things that happened during this period still impact on our lives in the twenty-first century. The influence of this period can be seen not only in the castles, churches and towns built at this time but also in our language, law and government and in how we relate to each other.

WHAT WAS IT LIKE TO LIVE IN IRELAND AT THIS TIME?

Ireland changed significantly after the Normans came. Government, society, the economy, religion and connections with the wider world had all changed by 1500. Throughout this chapter you are going to dig deeply, exploring what changed and what stayed the same over the period – don't forget to add to your concept map from Get Active 1 as you come across new information!

```
IMPORTANT CHANGES
    │
    ├──────────────┐
    ▼              ▼
IMPACT          IMPACT
ON PEOPLE        ON
OF THE TIME     TODAY
    │              │
    ▼              ▼
Christianity    Christianity
became          is still
the main        the main
established      established
religion         religion
```

1169		1500
Ireland was divided into a number of kingdoms which were ruled by Gaelic kings. There was one High King – Rory O'Connor.	Government ⟷	The Gaelic lords were weakened. The Normans were in control of a lot of Ireland and, by 1494, all Irish laws had to be approved by the King of England.
There was some social mobility – most people were peasants but could aspire to be nobles or kings if they were strong enough. Women were well protected by the law. Slavery was still common.	Society ⟷	The structure of society became more rigid. Women were less well off than they had been before. New styles of dress and customs were introduced. Slavery was forbidden.
People were relatively well-off. They worked to make their own food. There was little organised farming.	Economy ⟷	People remained relatively well-off. Organised farming was established and guilds to control trades were set up.
This was a mixture of Christianity and PAGANISM. There were many established monasteries, but people continued to believe in Celtic gods.	Religion ⟷	Christianity was well established. The Normans introduced the PARISH SYSTEM.
Ireland was an island but the Vikings had set up busy trading ports. Irish MISSIONARIES went to Britain and Europe.	Connections to the world ⟷	Trade and travel had increased. New towns were established and Ireland was trading with many European cities.

HOW WAS IRELAND GOVERNED IN 1169?

Ireland in 1169, showing the different kingdoms (in bold) and clans (in italics)

Government in pre-Norman Ireland was decided by the strength of one's army.

a Do you think this a good way to decide who should be in control of a country?

b If you were living in Ireland at this time would you have any say in who governed you? Explain your answer.

c Do people have enough say in how they are governed today? In what ways can they influence government?

In 1169, Ireland was divided into a number of different kingdoms, as shown in the map above. Each one was ruled by a different king. Among them, the king who could prove he was the strongest was known as the 'ard-ri' or High King. This meant that the kings of Ireland were constantly involved in conflict with each other, trying to take over each other's territory and become the most powerful. The kings themselves spent so long at war that often they could not rule their territories and had to employ governors to look after them. The last High King of Ireland was Rory O'Connor (see page 40).

HOW WAS IRELAND GOVERNED IN 1500?

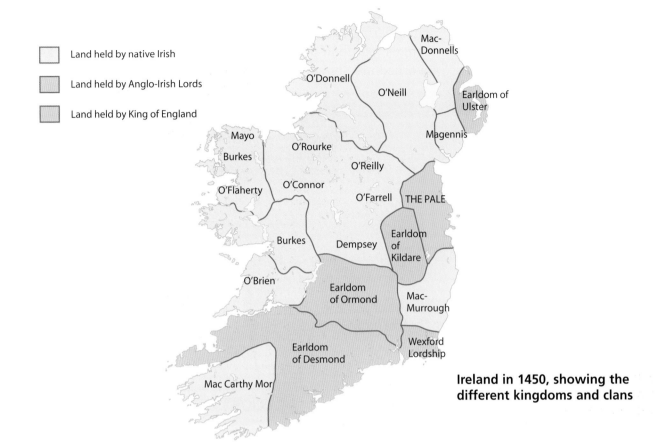

Land held by native Irish

Land held by Anglo-Irish Lords

Land held by King of England

Ireland in 1450, showing the different kingdoms and clans

By 1500, the Irish kings were no longer in control of the whole of Ireland. They were now sharing power with Norman lords. The map above shows how much land the Gaelic chiefs had lost. At first, after 1169, the Normans controlled large parts of Ireland, including the entire eastern coast. In 1171, King John became 'Lord of Ireland'.

By 1500, the Normans had both won and lost a lot of land in Ireland. John's successors, Henry III (1216–72) and Edward I (1272–1307) were more concerned with events in England, Wales, Scotland and Europe, which meant that the Normans in Ireland did not get much support from the English monarchy.

Wars between leading Norman families, the division of estates among heirs and the arrival of the Black Death in 1348 (see page 75) weakened the Normans' power. This allowed the Gaelic families to claim back some of the land they had lost. By 1500, the English were pushed back to the Pale, a small fortified area around Dublin. The English government based there did not have much real power any longer. Within the Pale, people lived in a manner similar to those of their counterparts in England, except that they were under constant threat of attack by the Irish. Outside the Pale, many Normans continued to live the Irish way of life.

GET ACTIVE 3

Study both maps. What do they show you about how government changed during this period? Do they show you whether anything stayed the same?

CHANGES IN GOVERNMENT 1169–1500

As we saw in Chapter 2, a timeline is a useful way of remembering events over a period of time to get an overview of changes that took place. The changes in the way Ireland was governed are shown in a timeline below.

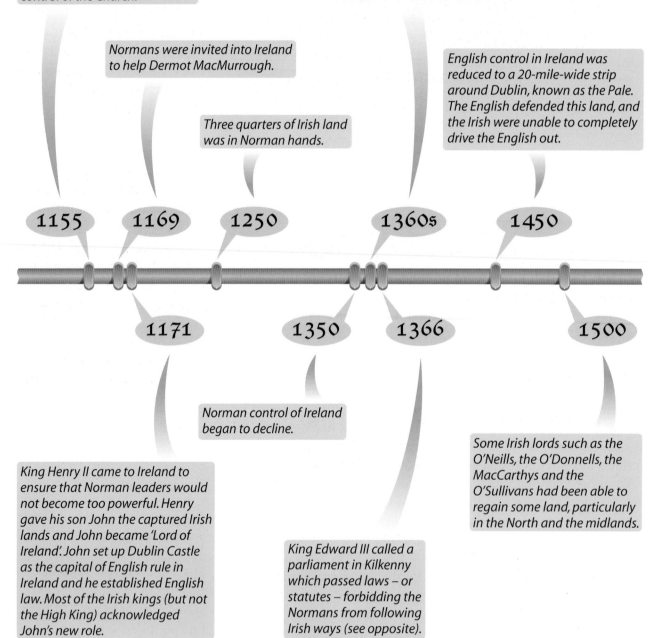

Pope Adrian IV encouraged King Henry II to invade Ireland. The Pope thought Henry could help him bring Ireland under the control of the Church.

King Edward III became alarmed about the extent to which the Normans adopted Irish laws, customs, dress and language.

Normans were invited into Ireland to help Dermot MacMurrough.

English control in Ireland was reduced to a 20-mile-wide strip around Dublin, known as the Pale. The English defended this land, and the Irish were unable to completely drive the English out.

Three quarters of Irish land was in Norman hands.

1155   **1169**   **1250**   **1360s**   **1450**

1171   **1350**   **1366**   **1500**

Norman control of Ireland began to decline.

King Henry II came to Ireland to ensure that Norman leaders would not become too powerful. Henry gave his son John the captured Irish lands and John became 'Lord of Ireland'. John set up Dublin Castle as the capital of English rule in Ireland and he established English law. Most of the Irish kings (but not the High King) acknowledged John's new role.

King Edward III called a parliament in Kilkenny which passed laws – or statutes – forbidding the Normans from following Irish ways (see opposite).

Some Irish lords such as the O'Neills, the O'Donnells, the MacCarthys and the O'Sullivans had been able to regain some land, particularly in the North and the midlands.

Statutes of Kilkenny

I   Settlers must not marry Irish natives.

II   Speaking the Irish language is forbidden.

III Irish modes of dress and other customs must be rejected.

Some of King Edward III's laws

GET ACTIVE 4

Have you ever heard the phrase 'beyond the pale'? What does the phrase mean? (If you haven't heard of the expression, use a dictionary or the internet to help you.) Can you explain the origin of this phrase?

GET ACTIVE 5

One way of recording feelings is to plot them on a 'living graph'. The example below shows how a living graph might look for someone just like you, like Rory from page 15.

- Create a similar graph which reflects the ups and downs in your life so far.
- Then create a new graph using the key dates that are given in the timeline on the page opposite. Map out on your graph how a Gaelic chieftain might have felt about these events. Then, using a different colour, map how a Norman might have felt.

Rory's living graph

1996 Had first birthday party

2001 Won medal at sports day

2000 Moved to primary school

2005 Was in school play

1998 Started nursery school

1995 Born

2000 Moved house, had to make new friends

2006 Started post primary school

1997 Gran was sick

2004 Was in hospital for a week!

51

HOW DID SOCIETY AND THE ECONOMY CHANGE?

How many people were there?

1169 – 500,000 people

1500 – 1 million people

How was society structured?

1169 – People were kings, noblemen or commoners, and it was possible for people to move within the last two groups.

1500 – The structure of society had not changed significantly. Where the Normans remained in control, the feudal system was still established, but this was not as tightly controlled as in England.

Where did people live?

1169 – Most people in Ireland lived in round huts in small rural settlements. The only towns were those established by the Vikings, such as Dublin, Waterford and Wexford. These were busy trading ports.

1500 – Most people lived in small rural villages. New towns such as Kilkenny, Athlone and Carrickfergus were established. Forests were cut down and some roads built to help transport goods, but most people did not venture beyond their locality.

What were living conditions like?

1169 – People in Ireland at this time were relatively well-off. All of their needs – for food, shelter and clothing – were met most of the time, although poverty did exist in the towns. Famine and disease were also evident from time to time in the bigger towns.

1500 – People continued to have enough for their needs. Exports of animal hides and other goods from the new towns brought some prosperity. Famine and disease still occurred, but mostly in urban areas.

What did people eat?

1169 – The diet consisted of corn, milk, fruit, vegetables and some meat – beef, pork and lamb and occasionally horsemeat. In the summer, vegetables such as onions, celery, leeks, cabbage and peas were eaten.

1500 – The basic diet remained the same, but increased trading links with European ports gave access to new goods such as spices and wine. Only wealthier people could afford these expensive new goods.

GET ACTIVE 6

a What does a person need to eat each day to ensure they have a balanced and healthy diet?

b Do you think the menu in 1500 would have been sufficient to ensure good health?

c Plan a menu for a day for a poor person living in Ireland in 1500.

d Draw up a list of what you ate yesterday. How does your diet compare with the menu that you planned for the person in 1500?

e Until very recently, most people were happy if their basic needs (for food, clothing and shelter) were met.
  • Would you be happy with this? Give reasons.
  • What else do people consider essential for happiness today?

f Look back at the concept map you created at the beginning of this chapter (page 46). Can you add any new information to it now from the information on these two pages?

HOW DID SOCIETY CHANGE? THE ROLE OF WOMEN

How were women treated in 1169?

While social, legal, political and cultural life in pre-Norman Ireland was dominated by men, as was the case in every other society in Europe at this time, women in Ireland seemed to have enjoyed greater freedom than their European counterparts.

In 1169, women were protected by the BREHON LAWS, which stated that:

a If a couple divorced, women were allowed to hold onto property they had brought to the marriage and also received half of any profits made during the marriage.

b Women could hold personal property, including land.

c Men were not allowed to mistreat their wives, or they would be punished.

d The Law of the Innocents of 697 stated that women, children and clergy could not be legitimate targets in times of war. This still applied in 1169.

How were women treated in 1500?

By 1500, life for women in Ireland had changed. As the Normans gained control over parts of Ireland, the Brehon Laws which had protected women fell into disuse. The medieval Church taught that a woman's role was to be a wife and a mother. As Christianity became more established, this view of women became increasingly accepted.

a Women could hold land, but this would become their husband's property whenever they married.

Women must obey and serve men …

b Women were paid less than men for doing the same jobs.

c Most women worked in the fields but some were involved in trades, such as spinning and weaving.

d The Church taught women they should be meek and obedient to their fathers or husbands.

GET ACTIVE 7

a Was life fair for women in Ireland in 1500? Draw up a list of the advantages and disadvantages of being a woman at this time.

b Was life better for women in 1500 than it had been in 1169, or did life get worse? Give reasons for your answer.

c Do women today – here and in other parts of the world – have a better deal than medieval Irish women? Explain your answer.

HOW DID SOCIETY CHANGE? SLAVERY

Slavery in 1169

In 1169, Irish society, like other European societies at the time, made use of slave labour. According to the *Annals*, which recorded events in Ireland up to the seventeenth century, children were sold into slavery by their parents when times were hard. In 965 and again in 1116, the *Annals* record that famines were so severe that fathers sold their children for food.

Slavery was also an important aspect of warfare. The *Annals* reveal that the Irish also made slaves of Vikings they defeated in battle. After internal battles, Irish kings sold PRISONERS OF WAR in the Dublin slave market and a thriving slave trade developed between Dublin and western Europe. Often, slaves were bought in England and brought back to Ireland to be sold on.

SOURCE 1

Bristol has an established slave market where slaves are brought from all over England for selling to Ireland. You might well groan to see the long rows of young men and maidens, whose beauty and youth might move the pity of the savage, bound together with cords, and brought to market to be sold.

William of Malmesbury, a historian who lived in the twelfth century

Slavery in 1500

By 1500, slavery had disappeared in Ireland. The influence of the Normans and the Church combined to make the practice virtually extinct. The Normans did not practise slave trading. It was banned in England when the Westminster Council of 1102 ruled that '*no one is henceforth to presume to carry on that shameful trading whereby heretofore men used in England to be sold like brute beasts.*' This was applied to Ireland.

Slavery in Ireland was condemned by the Church. At a meeting of the Irish bishops in Armagh after the Norman invasion, it was declared that the invasion was a punishment by God because the Irish had made slaves of other peoples.

SOURCE 2

The disaster struck [the Irish] by the stern judgement of God's vengeance. It had been their habit to buy Englishmen from merchants as well as from robbers and pirates and to make slaves of them. But now they in turn would be turned into slaves by that same race ...

Gerald of Wales writing in 1189 about the arrival of the Normans in Ireland

GET ACTIVE 8

a How and why did the slave trade in Ireland change between 1169 and 1500? Use both the sources and the text to help you answer this question.

b Do you think it was right for parents to sell their children at times of great famine? Is it ever right for parents to sell their children?

c Bonded labour is a type of slavery where people or their children have to work to pay off money that has been loaned to them. It exists in some less economically developed countries today, such as in the example in the photo below. Research the internet to produce a short report on the bonded labour of children. Your report should include details about where this happens and what conditions the children live and work in. The UNICEF website might be a good starting point for your research.

A child on a weaving chair in the silk and carpet factory in the Muslim area of the city of Varansi, India. Children in the developing world are often forced out of school to support themselves and their families.

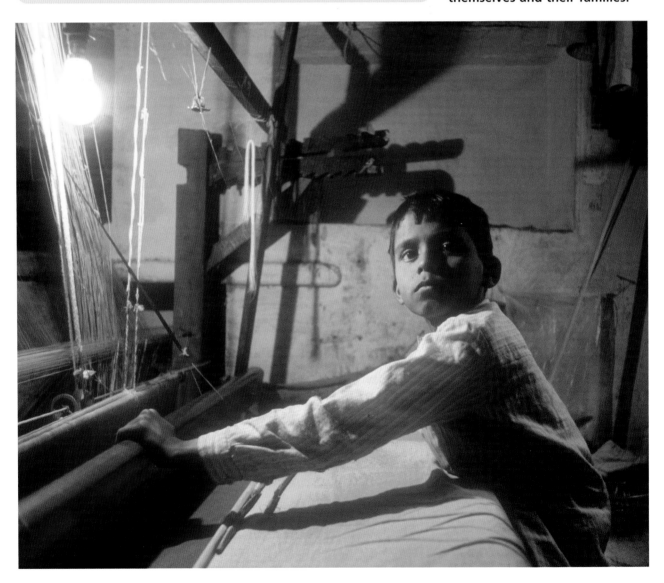

DID THE NORMANS STRENGTHEN OR WEAKEN THE CHURCH?

Religion in 1169

In 1169, religion in Ireland was a combination of Christianity and Celtic spirituality.

SOURCE 1

When they were asked if they were Christians and baptised, they replied that they had never heard of Christ.

Gerald of Wales, in 1189, writing about Irish people he encountered on his tour of Ireland with Prince John

SOURCE 2

Endeavour to enlarge the boundaries of the Church and reveal the truth of the Christian faith to ignorant and barbarous nations ... Encourage these people to have good morals, and plant the Christian religion and make it grow and you will obtain an abundant and lasting reward from God, and on earth a name glorious throughout the ages.

Papal Bull, 1155

CELTIC BELIEFS

Ancient Celtic beliefs had no fixed doctrine, but were linked to nature and based around oral legends.

The religious leaders of the Celts were known as Druids and they performed rituals and ceremonies, offered sacrifices, told fortunes, performed magic, gave advice on faith and morals, and acted as mediators between people and the gods.

The Celts believed in over 300 gods, most of whom had a connection to nature or to an aspect of life such as fertility or healing.

A number of religious festivals were celebrated in the Celtic calendar. One major Celtic festival was Bealtaine on 1 May, which celebrated crop planting and fertility. The feast of Samhain was celebrated on 1 November and this was a harvest festival, which marked the start of the New Year. On this night, the underworld of the dead supposedly opened up and spirits roamed the Earth. People carved faces in large turnips to scare away any evil spirits. Gods were honoured by lighting huge bonfires.

CHRISTIAN BELIEFS

Christianity existed alongside Celtic beliefs at this time and many people believed in elements of both. In the fifth century, St Patrick came to Ireland to preach to a small number of Christians and to begin to convert non-Christian people. Patrick incorporated some traditional Celtic rituals into his Christianity. For example, he used bonfires to celebrate Easter, since the Irish were used to honouring their gods with fire. By doing so, Patrick was successful in converting the Irish, and Christianity became established.

Religious orders of monks such as the Cistercians and the Augustinians founded abbeys. The abbeys were considered to be the most important and wealthiest part of the Church.

However, the Church was not well organised, and many ordinary people and chieftains did not follow its rules. Priests permitted divorce and people did not pay taxes to the Church. In 1155, Pope Adrian IV supported King Henry II's invasion of Ireland in the hope that it would strengthen Christianity and bring the Irish Church into line with the rest of Europe (see Source 2).

Religion in 1500

Christianity was well established in Ireland by this time. The Normans introduced the parish system. This divided the country up into areas which were looked after by bishops and priests. Everyone in the parish had to pay a tithe (a tax amounting to a tenth of their income) to support the clergy. Many Norman lords also gave land to religious orders to build monasteries. For example, John de Courcy brought the Cistercians to Ulster, founding Inch Abbey, near Downpatrick. New religious orders, such as the Dominicans and the Franciscans, also came to Ireland.

The Normans relied heavily on the bishops to help them rule Ireland. However, in parts of Ireland where the Irish remained strong, practices within the Church were very different from those which were taught by the Church in Rome. For example, priests often married, had children and owned property.

As Christianity became more established, fewer people worshipped the Celtic gods, although many of the Celtic festivals continued to be celebrated.

GET ACTIVE 9

a What changes did the Normans make to the Church? Think about the parish system, monasteries, how well the Church controlled the people and their ideas, the role of priests, and so on.

b Did the Normans strengthen or weaken the Church? Give reasons for your answer.

HOW WAS IRELAND CONNECTED TO THE MEDIEVAL WORLD?

Today, the world seems a small place. You can fly to Australia in less than a day. You can chat to people on the other side of the world. Information about every country is at your fingertips. This wasn't always the case. In 1169, most people living in Ireland were unaware of what went on outside their settlement. However, long before the Normans arrived, Ireland was connected to Europe by trading routes and through the work of missionaries. Before the Normans arrived in 1169, Ireland and Britain were already co-operating in sharing and exchanging ideas, goods and services.

GET ACTIVE 10

a In small groups, talk about places you have visited outside of your own locality. Then, think about what you wear, eat and entertain yourself with.

- Were these things made locally, in Ireland or Britain, in Europe or elsewhere in the world?
- What does this tell you about how you are connected to people outside your own locality?
- Is this similar or different to people in 1169?

b As the map on page 61 shows, Britain and Ireland were connected in a number of different ways before 1169. Which were advantages and disadvantages for Ireland? Present your answer in a table like the one shown below.

Connection	Advantage	Disadvantage	Reason
Ireland exported goods to Britain.	✓		This meant that Ireland had income which could be spent on other things …

Britain and Ireland before 1169

From Britain to Ireland

From Ireland to Britain

Both ways

SCOTLAND

Scottish settlers came to Ireland to work as mercenaries for Gaelic lords. They were often rewarded with grants of land.

Irish monks such as St Colmcille and St Aidan went to England and Scotland to preach the gospel.

Ireland imported iron, salt and horses from Britain. Ireland exported leather, wool and clothing to Britain.

IRELAND

Ireland traded in slaves. Traders raided Britain to capture slaves for selling. St Patrick came to Ireland in AD432 as a slave.

Irish colonies were established in Wales and Scotland.

ENGLAND

WALES

AD500–800 was a golden age of learning in Ireland. English nobles went to Ireland to study at the monasteries.

GROWING CONNECTIONS 1169–1500

Between 1169 and 1500, Ireland's connections with Britain and Europe became more developed. Forests were cleared, making space to build roads and bridges all over Ireland. New towns such as Carrickfergus, Ardglass and Carlingford were established on the coast. This all made communication much easier. Trading links were established with European cities such as Bruges, Nantes, Bilbao, Oporto and Lisbon. Developments outside Ireland, such as the invention of the printing press and new ship designs, also improved communication.

Towns such as Carlingford grew as trading with the outside world developed. It still has a medieval appearance today.

How did people in Britain feel about their connections with Ireland?

SOURCE 1

The Irish are a barbarous race. They have a primitive lifestyle. Although the island they inhabit is rich in pastures, good fishing and hunting, enjoying an excellent climate free of disease and infestation, the inhabitants are too lazy to exploit its potential. Their clothes, their appearance and fashions are odd to say the least. Their customs and practices are barbarous and repugnant to all civilised people.

Gerald of Wales, The Conquest of Ireland, *1189*

SOURCE 2

After a short time, there was no deserted spot, almost no corner of land or place in the island, however remote, which was not filled up with holy monks and nuns, so that Ireland was quite rightly given throughout the world, the special name 'Island of Saints'.

Written in the 1180s by Jocelin, an English monk

SOURCE 3

Artefacts which survive from this time – manuscripts, precious metalwork objects such as jewellery, altar vessels and ornamental book covers – are relics of a society that was well organised and wealthy. This society must have compared favourably with other parts of western Europe.

Written by Sean Duffy, a contemporary historian, in his book Ireland in the Middle Ages, *1997*

GET ACTIVE 11

a Remember the 'W5' method you learned about in Chapter 4 (page 42) for judging the reliability and usefulness of sources? Use this to help you answer the following questions.
  • How do Gerald and Jocelin's views of the Irish differ?
  • Are Sources 1 and 2 more believable than Source 3? Explain your answer.
b The arrival of the Normans in 1169 has long been regarded as the start of conflict between the Irish and the English. Using your knowledge of connections before 1169, do you think this is a fair comment?

Plan, Do, Review

HOW DID LIFE IN IRELAND CHANGE DURING 1169–1500?

In this chapter, you have been trying to answer this question by looking at aspects of Ireland's government, society, economy and connections with the wider world and how these had changed (or stayed the same) by 1500.

Your task now is to work in groups to create a presentation on change in Ireland over the period 1169–1500. You could create a poster, use PowerPoint or present your learning in some other way. Your work must contain three visual images, three key words and three short pieces of text which, together, will show an interpretation of continuity and change after the Norman invasion.

Your work must also include your views on the following:

● What were the key changes over the period?
● What were the key things that stayed the same?
● What were the benefits of Norman settlement in Ireland?
● Did any aspect of life in Ireland get worse as a result of Norman settlement?

PLAN

Stage 1 – Decide on the format
Discuss the range of possibilities for your presentation:

● How might you each present your individual work?
● What are the advantages and disadvantages of each type of presentation?
● What is your personal preference?
● What type of work are you good at?

Consider all these factors and decide which type of presentation will work best for your group.

Stage 2 – Summarise the information
This chapter has focussed on changes in Ireland between 1169 and 1500 in:

● government
● society
● economy
● religion
● connections to the world.

Go back over the chapter and pick out a fact for each of these headings in 1169 and again in 1500.

Stage 3 – Make some judgments

You should now have a summary of the key developments over the period. So you need to decide:

- What were the main changes?
- What were the main things that stayed the same?
- What benefits did the Normans bring?
- Did any aspect of life get worse?

DO

- Create your presentation in your chosen format. Don't forget you are giving your group's interpretation of what the key changes were.
- Present your work to the class.

REVIEW

Does your presentation meet all the criteria?
- Does it contain three visual images, three key words and three short pieces of text?
- Did you include information on what changed and on what stayed the same?
- Did you give your view on what the benefits of Norman settlement in Ireland were and on whether any aspect of life in Ireland got worse as a result of Norman settlement?

6 Who was who in medieval Ireland?

In this chapter we are learning to:
- ✓ investigate inequalities in medieval Ireland;
- ✓ use empathy to find out about the experiences of different types of people in medieval Ireland;
- ✓ work with others to plan a documentary about the different people who were included and excluded in medieval Ireland.

History is about finding out what people thought and felt in the past. This is called EMPATHY. You do not just use your imagination when thinking about how people felt in the past. It is important to use different sources of information. We call this EVIDENCE. As you read through this chapter you will find out that some people were the 'haves' and others were the 'have-nots' in medieval society. This means that some of them were included in society whereas others found themselves excluded because of their DISABILITY, ETHNICITY or MATERIAL CIRCUMSTANCES.

GET ACTIVE 1

a Like today, medieval society had different types of people. Over pages 67–71 you will meet who was who in medieval Ireland. As you meet each character, try to think about who were the most important people and who was treated as the least important. Place the characters on a pyramid with the most important at the top and the least important at the bottom. Compare your pyramid with a partner.

b • In groups, make an information-gathering grid like the one below.
• Select phrases from the information and sources given on pages 67–71 to show the experiences of people in medieval society. An example is completed for you.

Type of person	Included/Excluded	Experiences	Evidence
King	Included	• most important person in society • called parliament if he wanted to raise taxes • listened to advice of barons and bishops • 'he was not afraid of God or any man'	Source 1

INTRODUCING ...

THE KING AND THE KING'S JUSTICIAR

I am the most important person in society. I make most of the decisions and own most of the land. Sometimes I listen to the advice of my barons and bishops. I call parliament when I want to and only when I need to get them to agree to me raising taxes.

Let me introduce my JUSTICIAR, who is my representative in Ireland. After all, I must make sure that the Norman lords in Ireland are obeying all my commands. The Justiciar is the most important judge in Ireland and commands my army in Ireland.

SOURCE 1

No one could stop the King from doing exactly what he wanted. He seemed to be the only powerful person in the country, and he was not afraid of God or any man.

Gervase, a monk from Canterbury, in Kent, England, in the early thirteenth century.

THE BARON

My name is Hugh de Lacy, and I have been given lots of land from the King of England in Meath. The king cannot rule the country properly without the help of us BARONS. We are very powerful because we have our own armies and can take control of certain areas. In order to keep control, however, we have to promise loyalty to the king and give him soldiers when needed.

SOURCE 2

At Oxford [in 1258], the barons still insisted that the king [Henry III] obey the Magna Carta, which his father had agreed to [and which Henry had ignored]. The barons also demanded that the officials be chosen to put right what the king had done wrong.

Matthew Paris, a monk from the monastery at St Albans, near London, in 1258.

THE BISHOP

As a BISHOP, I am one of the important people who control the Church. Religion is very important to people because they want to make sure they will get to heaven when they die. This gives us bishops a lot of power. People give money to the Church and want to obey what the Church says. The Normans in Ireland want bishops to be their own men rather than Irishmen. There have been orders from the King of England that no Irishman should be a bishop. I have heard, however, that in areas where the Normans have little control, Irishmen have become bishops.

SOURCE 3

Archbishop Becket is the next most important person to the King. When he crosses the English channel, he never has less than six ships. Every day he gives away valuable presents of horses, birds, clothes, gold, silver and money.

William Fitzstephen, a clerk of Archbishop Thomas Becket in 1170

LORD OF THE MANOR

As LORD OF THE MANOR, I have been given land by one of the great barons, Hugh de Lacy. In return for my land, I provide soldiers when he needs them. I own a castle and the land around my castle is my demesne. I have given out the rest of my land to the peasants in strips. This means that the peasants pay me rent and provide labour on my demesne.

SOURCE 4

I will be your man from this day onwards. I shall be true and faithful to you for the lands I hold from you.

Oath of allegiance from the eleventh century. The Lord of the Manor would have sworn this to the baron.

PEASANTS

In Ireland we peasants are called BETAGHS. Before the Normans came, we were free men and women, but we are now the property of each Norman lord who owns the land. We are treated like the serfs in England. As John Ball, a poor priest preaching during the Peasant's Revolt in the year of our Lord 1381, said: 'we are called slaves and unless we do as we are told we get beaten'. The Norman lords are finding that there are not enough betaghs to work their land and so they have persuaded peasants from Wales and England to settle in Ireland. Some of these peasants were serfs but they have been given their freedom in Ireland. They are treated better than us, yet we are native to the island of Ireland.

SOURCE 5

Peasants reaping the harvest supervised by the Lord's official, dated 1300–1325

Attention all betaghs!

Rules from the Lord of the Manor

I. When you take over land, you must pay tax to me.

II. When you die, your family have to give me one of your best animals as a tax.

III. You have to pay me a special payment called a 'merchet' when you get married.

IV. You cannot leave the village without my permission.

THE POOR

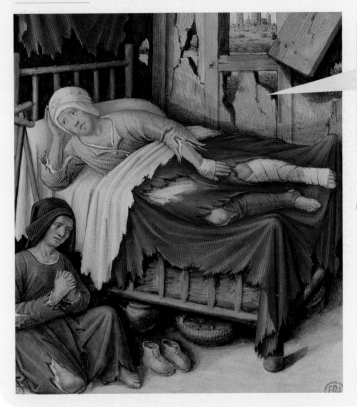

What I earn from spinning, I have to spend on feeding my children and the rent for my home. I am so poor! I myself often have to go hungry. There is misery in the winter because I have to get up in the night to rock my children's cradle, wash, dress the family and wind woollen thread. The misery of women like me who dwell in these hovels is too sad to speak of.

SOURCE 6

As I went along I saw a poor man
  ploughing.
At the end of the field was a baby in
  rags and two 2-year olds.
The children cried all the time.

From a fourteenth century poem

What a poor person's home would have been like around 1500

THE SICK

I am treated as an outcast because people are scared of catching leprosy and because lepers are so badly disfigured. This dreadful disease is seen as a divine punishment for sin. We are kept separate from the healthy. Thankfully, hospitals for lepers run by monks have opened on the outskirts of towns all over the country.

SOURCE 7

Medieval people did not know about germs – so they could not know that germs called illness. If they could not see the reason for the illness, they often assumed it was a punishment from God.

From Medieval Realms, *a history textbook by J F Aylett, written in 1991*

THE DISABLED

I am a cripple who was born with this infirmity. People look down on me. They think I am the way I am because God is punishing me for my sin. No one helps me and I am forced to beg at the gate of the church. Thankfully, some nuns have given me food and a place to sleep for the past few nights.

SOURCE 8

In medieval times, people treated disabled persons as heretics, works of the devil, or outcasts. When plagues broke out, they were often used as scapegoats and viewed as evil people who brought disasters.

Adapted from a website about the History of Disabled Persons, *written by J Barrett.*

THE JEWS

I work as a money lender in Ireland. Some of my fellow Jews get badly treated and occasionally murdered by Christian mobs. King Edward II forced the Jews to leave England in 1290.

SOURCE 9

The leaders of the Jews arrived, against the orders of the King. The King's men seized the Jews, stripped them, flogged them and threw them out. Some they killed. Others they let go half dead. However, the people of London, hearing this, turned on the Jews of the city and robbed them and killed many of both sexes. They set light to their houses and razed them to ashes.

Events at King Richard I's coronation in 1189 described by a medieval writer

Plan, Do, Review

WHO WAS WHO IN MEDIEVAL IRELAND?

In this chapter you have found out about who was who in medieval Ireland. You have explored the different people who were included in society and those who were excluded. You have been able to use your empathy skills to find out about the different experiences of these different types of people from the past.

In groups, your task is to create a ten-minute TV programme about who was who in medieval Ireland explaining who was included and who was excluded.

PLAN

Stage 1

- Re-read your information-gathering grid from page 66 about those included and excluded in medieval society.
- In order to produce a TV programme that is interesting for your viewers, you will need to have actors re-enacting some of the different types of people from medieval society. Re-read the character cards on pages 67–71. Who will you choose: king, leper or peasant ... ?
  - Choose to interview two of the important people in medieval society.
  - Choose to interview two of the people who felt excluded in medieval society.

Stage 2

Decide who is to be:

- The presenter of the TV programme. This person who will introduce the programme and make links between the interviews. The presenter needs to plan what he or she is going to say.
- Interviewers. They will need to ask specific questions to different people living in medieval Ireland. The interviewers will need to plan their questions and let the interviewees know what they will be asked.
- The four different characters you have chosen to be interviewed. They will need to think about what life would have been like for them and how they were treated by others.

DO

Bring your TV programme together with each group member performing his or her task as a presenter, interviewer or character. You will have to practise it a number of times. You may want to video it. Perform your programme to the rest of the class.

REVIEW

Each group will assess the different TV programmes made by the other groups. Your class can decide the criteria by which your TV programme will be assessed. An example is given for you in the table below:

	Poor 1	Satisfactory 2	Good 3	Very Good 4	Excellent 5
Content of the programme – did you learn about four people who lived in medieval Ireland?					
Presentation – was the programme interesting?					
Working with others – how well did the group work together? Was everyone involved?					

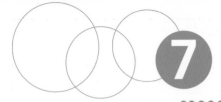

7 What were health and medicine like in the Middle Ages?

In this chapter we are learning to:
- ✓ find out why people in the Middle Ages could not stop diseases from spreading;
- ✓ write an essay explaining what health and medicine were like in the Middle Ages.

In the Middle Ages, medical knowledge was very basic and most people believed the Church's theory that ill health was a punishment from God. Common causes of death were influenza, diarrhoea, blood poisoning and infections from childbirth.

THE BLACK DEATH

Because of the lack of knowledge about what caused disease, contagious diseases would spread very quickly. In the fourteenth century, the BUBONIC PLAGUE spread throughout Europe. The bubonic plague was named after the large black swellings (or buboes) as big as an egg which appeared under people's armpits. These lumps were followed by red and black spots all over the body. It was an incredibly painful and slow death, so people called it the BLACK DEATH. As it crossed Europe, it killed one in every three people.

The disease came to Ireland in 1349. Infected rats had carried it on ships from overseas. In some areas, it killed up to 90 per cent of the population. In Ireland it spread from the port in Dublin to towns like Drogheda and Kilkenny.

I helped spread the plague because the fleas on my back sucked my blood, which contained plague germs. When the fleas bit humans, the plague germs went into their blood stream. Nobody in the Middle Ages knew about this.

GET ACTIVE 1

a Use the map on page 75 to write down the names of the countries in Europe that were affected by the Black Death.

b The word 'EPIDEMIC' refers to a disease which spreads across a particular area affecting many people. Do you think the Black Death could be described as an epidemic? Give reasons.

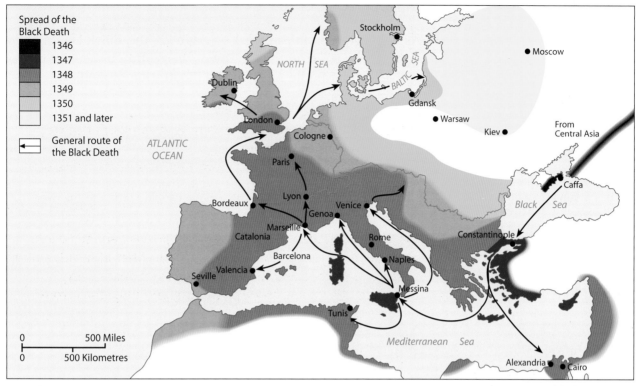

Map showing the journey of the Black Death across Europe to Ireland

SOURCE 1

Plague stripped villages, cities, castles and towns of their inhabitants so thoroughly, that there was scarcely anyone left alive in them. The pestilence was so contagious that those who touched the dead or the sick were immediately affected themselves and died. The penitent and confessor were carried together to the grave. Because of their fear and horror, men could hardly bring themselves to perform the pious and charitable acts of visiting the sick and burying the dead. Many died of boils, abscesses and pustules which erupted on the legs and in the armpits. Others died in frenzy, brought on by an affliction of the head, or vomiting blood ... It was very rare for just one person to die in a house, usually, husband, wife, children and servants all went the same way, the way of death.

And I, Brother John Clyn of the Friars Minor in Kilkenny ... seeing these many ills, and that the whole world is encompassed by evil, waiting among the dead for death to come ... leave parchment for continuing the work, in case anyone should still be alive in the future and any son of Adam can escape this pestilence and continue the work thus begun.

[Here the narrative breaks off and is followed by a note in another hand:]

Here, it seems, the author died.

Brother Clyn's account of what happened in the town of Kilkenny after the plague arrived. The account comes from the Kilkenny Chronicles.

GET ACTIVE 2

a Do you think Brother Clyn in Source 1 had a good understanding of what caused the plague? Explain your answer.

b How did you react to Source 1? Is the way that it was written important in making it memorable? Pick out one or two sentences or phrases that had an effect on you and explain why they did.

DEADLY TOWNS

As we have seen in Source 1 on page 75, the Black Death had a devastating effect in towns. Towns were often unhealthy places to live in the Middle Ages, as the illustration of medieval Dublin shows.

2. Wells for drinking water and cesspools for sewage were often next to each other.

1. Rats lived off rubbish and burrowed into wooden houses and thatched roofs.

3. There were open sewers carrying refuse to the river.

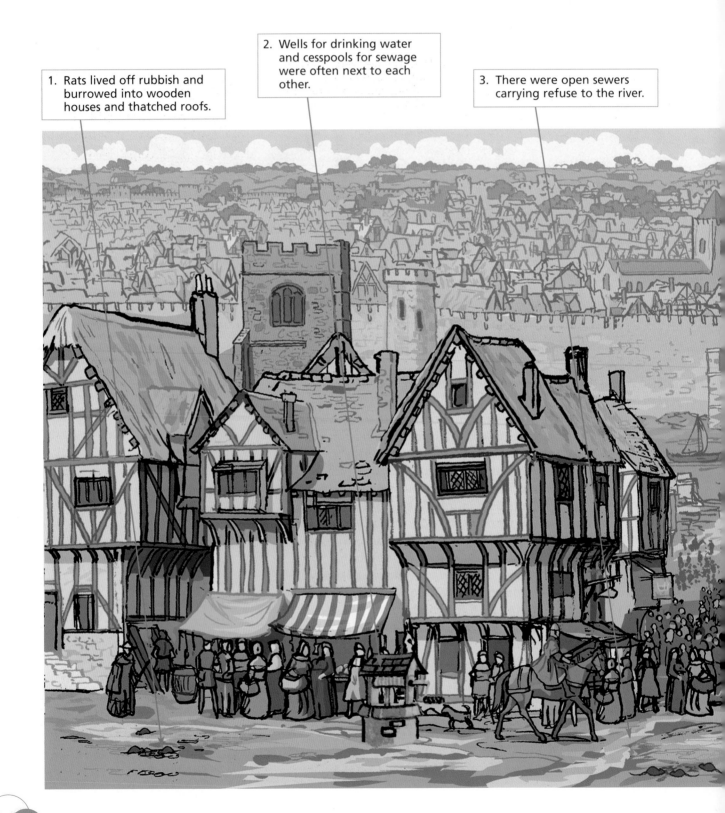

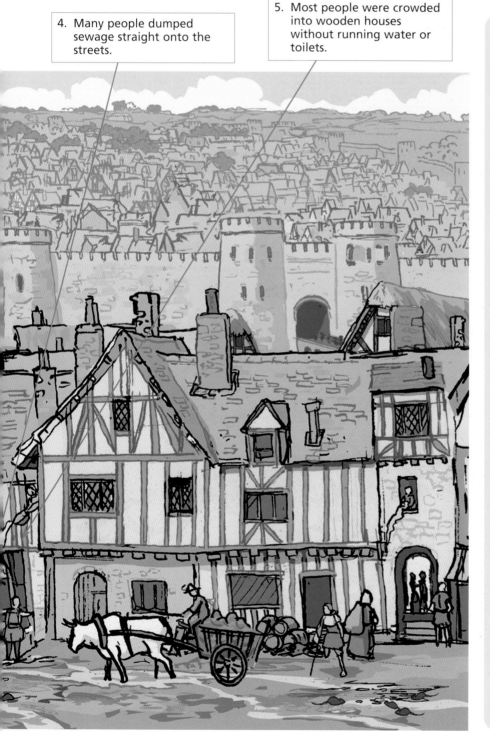

4. Many people dumped sewage straight onto the streets.

5. Most people were crowded into wooden houses without running water or toilets.

GET ACTIVE 3

a Get into groups of four and number the people in your group 1 to 4.

b Number 1 should look at the picture on these two pages for 20 seconds and then close the book.

c Number 1 should then draw what they can remember on an A3 sheet of paper.

d Then, number 2 should look at the picture for 20 seconds and add to the picture started by number 1. Continue until all four members of your group have done the same. What you will have created together is a memory map.

e Once you have your memory map, compare it to the picture in the book. Is there anything vital missing from your map? If so, add it now.

f What have you learned from creating your map that you didn't know before?

g Write a few sentences explaining why living in towns such as the one in the drawing would have made people's lives unhealthy.

HOW DID PEOPLE EXPLAIN DISEASE?

Medicine in the Middle Ages could not help to stop the plague epidemic. Doctors did not know what was causing it. Understanding of the causes and the treatments for illness or disease were mostly based on superstitions and tradition, as these sources show.

SOURCE 1

The general cause was the close position of the three great planets, Saturn, Jupiter and Mars. This had taken place in 1345 on 24 March, in the fourteenth degree of Aquarius. Such a coming together of planets is always a sign of wonderful, terrible or violent things to come.

Guy de Chauliac, a French doctor writing in his book called Surgery *about the cause of the plague epidemic* in the fourteenth century

SOURCE 2

Against toothache, take a candle and burn it close to the tooth. The worms that are gnawing the tooth will fall out into the water.

A medieval cure for toothache, dated fourteenth century

SOURCE 3

Cause the human faeces and other filth lying in the streets and lanes in the city to be removed with all speed to places far distant, so that no greater cause of mortality may arise from such smells.

From a letter from King Edward III to the Mayor of London in 1349

SOURCE 4

Flagellants whipping themselves. Flagellants believed that the Black Death was sent by God to punish people for committing sin. They punished themselves in public, hoping for God's forgiveness.

SOURCE 5

A fourteenth century doctor drawing blood from a patient's arm

GET ACTIVE 2

a Sources 1–5 all tell us something about health or medicine in the Middle Ages. For each source, write a phrase, word or sentence which best describes the information in that source.

b What can you learn from the sources about:
 • medical practice at the time;
 • the influence of superstition on people's beliefs?

Plan, Do, Review

WHAT WERE HEALTH AND MEDICINE LIKE IN THE MIDDLE AGES?

In this chapter we have been trying to answer this question by looking at information about:

● how diseases like the Black Death spread;
● how unhealthy life was in towns;
● how medieval people's explanations of disease were wrong and didn't help to prevent epidemics.

Your task is to turn this information into a essay with the title: 'What were health and medicine like in the Middle Ages?'

PLAN

Your essay should contain:

● an introduction;
● paragraphs explaining each different aspect of health and medicine at the time;
● a conclusion in which you make an overall statement.

Stage 1 – Decide what to write in your introduction
Re-read Chapter 7 to get the big picture. Write down a sentence that sums up what you are going to say. For example, 'It was hard for people in the Middle Ages to stay healthy because ...'

Stage 2 – Decide what to write in each paragraph
Choose one particular aspect of the information in the chapter, for example, how diseases like the Black Death spread. Add an example and then explain what this told you about medieval health and medicine. Once you have planned one paragraph, repeat the style for a different aspect. Make sure you connect your paragraphs by using words or phrases like: 'another aspect was', 'another reason why' or 'furthermore'.

Stage 3 – Decide what to write in your conclusion
This is where you will pull your ideas together and make a statement where you may add your own ideas, for example, 'Health and medicine in the Middle Ages were not very advanced compared to today.'

DO

Write your essay using this writing frame to help you.

> **Introduction**
> Health and medicine in the Middle Ages were …
>
> **First paragraph**
> The spread of diseases …
>
> **Second paragraph**
> The causes of diseases such as the Black Death were explained in different ways. For example …
>
> **Third paragraph**
> As people didn't know what caused disease, they lived unhealthy lives in towns. For example …
>
> **Conclusion**
> Overall, health and medicine in the Middle Ages were …

REVIEW

1. Choose a partner and take turns reading each other's essay. Tell each other how similar or different your ideas and arguments were.
2. Decide together what makes a good essay. Here are some ideas which may help you to decide:

- Good introduction;
- Well-informed explanations;
- Connecting words between each paragraph;
- Good plan;
- Ideas organised into paragraphs;
- Interesting conclusion;
- Answers the question asked.

3. Were any of the above points missing in your essay?
4. What would you do differently the next time you write an essay?

8 Did the Normans leave us anything worth keeping?

In this chapter we are learning to:
✓ select, organise and present information about the Norman legacy;
✓ work with others to create a flier about Carrickfergus Castle.

WHAT DID THE NORMANS LEAVE BEHIND?

As we have seen in Chapter 5, by the fourteenth century the power and influence of the Normans in Ireland had declined. However, they have left behind a legacy in many aspects of life today. These are part of our heritage and the diagram below shows some of them.

Trim Castle, Co. Meath, built by King John in 1220, is one of the largest and best preserved Anglo- Norman castles in Ireland.

LANGUAGE

SOURCE 1

Many of the English nation have become like Irishmen, and now send their children among the Irish to be nursed and taught the Irish tongue … People of the English race have become Irish.

Royal Decree from the King of England in 1360

Many of our everyday words come from the Norman language, such as 'beef' (boeuf) and 'pork' (porc).

BURKE

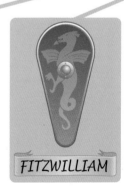
FITZWILLIAM

GET ACTIVE 1

a With a partner, think of at least three reasons why some aspects of the Norman legacy might be more important than others. For example, 'the Normans improved the local economy' might be a reason. Rank your reasons in order.

b The reasons you ranked in part a) can now be used as criteria to decide how important each aspect of the Norman legacy in the diagram below is. List the aspects and rank them in order of importance according to how well they meet your reasons from part a). Feedback your ideas to the class.

c Then, take a class vote to decide on the order the aspects of Norman legacy should go in.

d Read Source 1. Some historians have said that the Normans in Ireland became more Irish than the Irish themselves. So, by the fourteenth century, Norman lords had become GAELICISED. Do you think this would have weakened or strengthened the Norman legacy in Ireland? Give reasons for your answer.

BUILDINGS

WHAT DID THE NORMANS LEAVE BEHIND THEM IN IRELAND?

SURNAMES OF NORMAN ORIGIN

TOWNS

Inch Abbey in Downpatrick is a **CISTERCIAN** abbey built by John De Courcy in 1180 and is the first building in Ireland to be built with Gothic arches.

LYNCH   BUTLER

Carlingford, built by Hugh De Lacy in the twelfth century, is one of the best preserved Norman towns in Ireland. It was given its first charter in 1326 by Edward II.